D1491281

Praise for *Leaders Ope.*

"Through richly entertaining stories and to-the-point tips, *Leaders Open Doors* gets to the heart of what matters most about leadership: creating opportunities for others."

Laurie Ann Goldman
CEO, SPANX

"*Leaders Open Doors* is an amazing book! With a gazillion leadership books available, Bill Treasurer brings a power-ful, practical treatment that uniquely reframes a quality still in short supply. Written with refreshing clarity, delight-ful humor, and profound insight, the book is a must-read for all interested in successfully influencing others to deliver their best."

Chip R. Bell
author of *Managers as Mentors*

"Bill Treasurer has broken new ground with *Leaders Open Doors*. This exceptional book provides a simple yet authen-tic and powerful roadmap for leadership mastery."

Chris Maslin
director of staffing and training, The Biltmore Company

"Yes, you can teach old dogs new tricks! If you think you've had your fill of leadership tomes, tricks, and tools . . . don't walk away. Bill's wonderful ability to use word pictures and genuine and realistic examples makes this a wonderful treat . . . one that teaches anyone, anywhere!"

Beverly Kaye
founder and co-CEO, Career Systems International
co-author of *Help Them Grow or Watch Them Go: Career Conversations Employees Want*

"Are you an open-door leader? The concept is simple but powerful. Read this book to find out how you can open doors and create more opportunities for yourself as a leader, those you lead, and your organization."

Mark Sanborn
president, Sanborn & Associates
author of *The Fred Factor*

"In a simple yet powerful way, *Leaders Open Doors* practices what it teaches! It opens the door to what makes leaders effective and leaves the reader with an array of practical suggestions to improve one's own capability as a leader. Kudos to Bill for getting to the heart of the matter in a way we can all use to become better leaders."

Tony Scotto
EVP and chief development officer, ACI Worldwide, Inc.

"So you hope your talent will stay engaged and producing at their peak, right? Bill Treasurer tells you exactly how to do that by simply opening six unique opportunity doors in ways that help people stretch and grow. His charming, profound stories will keep you turning the pages while they illustrate how to 'lighten your leadership load' and delight your valuable employees."

Sharon Jordan-Evans
president, Jordan Evans Group
co-author, *Love 'Em or Lose 'Em:*
Getting Good People to Stay

"In this highly readable book, Bill Treasurer brings leadership out of vague idealist generalities and makes it tangible, clear, and practical. The steps of leadership are not hard, but that doesn't make leadership easy. *Leaders Open Doors* points out how we can each choose the path of leadership in our own lives."

Conor Neill
visiting professor, IESE Business School
past area-director, Entrepreneurs' Organization

"*Leaders Open Doors* does what every good leadership book should: deliver a keyleadership concept, illustrate and support it with real-world examples, and offer solid suggestions for how to implement it. . . . This little leadership book is a gem worth reading."

Barry Silverstein
ForeWord Reviews

Leaders
Open Doors

2nd Edition

A Radically Simple Leadership Approach
to Lift People, Profits, and Performance

Bill Treasurer

Foreword by Jeff Carr

ATD Press is an internationally renowned source of insightful
and practical information on talent development, training, and
professional development.

ATD Press
1640 King Street
Alexandria, VA 22314 USA

Ordering information: Books published by ATD Press can be
purchased by visiting ATD's website at www.td.org/books or
by calling 800.628.2783 or 703.683.8100.

Library of Congress Control Number: 2014935110

ISBN 978-1-56286-964-9 (hardcover)
ISBN 978-1-56286-857-4 (pbk)
ISBN 978-1-60728-412-3 (electronic)

ASTD Press Editorial Staff:
Director: Glenn Saltzman
Manager, ASTD Press: Ashley McDonald
Community of Practice Manager, Human Capital: Ann Parker
Associate Editor: Melissa Jones
Editorial Assistant: Ashley Slade
Cover Design: Faceout Studio, Jeff Miller
Text Design: Lon Levy

Printed by Sheridan Books, Inc., Ann Arbor, Michigan,
www.sheridan.com

To all the open-door leaders who helped me believe in myself, especially Henry L. Thompson, Bob Carr, Hines Brannan, Ft. Vince Malatesta, and O.K. Sheffield.

One hundred percent of the author's royalties from the sales of this book are being donated to organizations that provide opportunities for children with special needs.

Contents

Foreword

I was exposed to open-door leadership early in my career. In this style of leadership, decisions are made openly and determined by capability. Managers solve problems through enablement and empowerment.

My earliest views toward leadership were formed by these open-door leadership models. I learned how work got done from some of the best—I learned that great leadership is not hierarchical, but rather dependent on people who are willing and able to lead an initiative to a desired outcome. This is the very message that drives *Leaders Open Doors*.

As Bill Treasurer so succinctly explains, effective leadership can only be grown in a setting where doors are opened, creativity and innovation are requirements, and employees stretch their own abilities and push against the organization's comfort zone. Solving problems is a small scale, closed-door approach. An open-door leader must focus on the outcome and opening the doors of opportunity to those that he or she employs.

This kind of outcome-focused thinking has helped me see that leadership is itinerant and dependent. You could say that my job is often to foster a collaborative, transparent, energized environment—one where people can step up to and into leadership opportunities, not because of their titles or who they know, but because of what they can do to help our stakeholders, our people, and our customers succeed.

I wish I was ingenious enough to think of this approach all by myself, but like Bill, who was inspired by his five-year-old child, I came to this realization by listening to and learning from others. Early in my career I worked for an organization that taught me the importance of advocating for our customers' desired outcomes. I discovered that obstacles were opportunities and learned to value them. This was once clearly illustrated to me when I worked with my colleague, Max. He was not someone I managed; like me, he managed another team.

Max had just lost a series of deals. I caught him staring out of his office window, withdrawn, head down. He looked dejected. I knocked and, without asking, walked in. We started to talk and he described his tremendous sense of failure. I just watched Max and nodded. When he was done, I asked three simple questions: "How do you think your team feels?" "How do you think your manager feels?" "How are those prospects' lives going to be affected when they deploy the lesser solutions?"

Anyone can lead when things look bright. But, how we act during difficult times really defines us. Leaders aren't successful at leading because they win every time—they are defined by who they are and how they serve others when they fail. Failure is part of the game and right then Max's team needed strength and support, not feelings of weakness and failure. They needed to know he believed in them.

Max had an opportunity in front of him. He had the opportunity to change the situation from one where failure ruled to one where he led a team away from failure and opened doors to new ideas, new motivations, and new starts. He had to accept the situation and move forward, otherwise he was closing doors, wallowing in the problem, and blinding himself and others to the new opportunities ahead.

I realize now more than ever the value of this open-door leadership style. It starts by looking, feeling, and listening. True leaders can learn about a problem simply by observing the situation. They can then use their insights to determine a solution. As Bill says in this book, by focusing on opportunities we can create the conditions we want.

Opportunities beget opportunity. We live by this at Peoplefluent. By focusing on "socializing" learning, recruiting, talent and leadership development, we continue to open doors to new ideas, thought leadership, and conversations. Even our products encourage people to lead rather than manage, and share successes rather than focus on failure. We empower collaboration by helping to create transparency and increase communication. We assist organizations in finding and hiring the best people so their teams have the best chance for success. I like to think that what we do and what we offer opens doors for others to step into roles of leadership, creativity, and prosperity.

Nothing can replace the fundamental tenets of a service-based leadership approach. And this message is at the heart of Bill's open-door leadership model. We open doors to be kind and to help others, but we also open doors to let people in and to provide an entry point for our colleagues who might not have known where to go. Open-door leadership is a lifestyle, not an event. May the next door you open provide entry to a new world for the people you serve—whether for a friend, colleague, employee, manager, or even family member.

Leaders Open Doors affirms the best thinking about leadership. I see in Bill and this book a simple and clear message—leaders don't measure success in terms of themselves; leaders measure success in terms of the outcomes they help other others achieve.

Jeff Carr
CEO, Peoplefluent

Preface

My five-year-old son Ian is a preschooler at the Asheville Montessori School in Asheville, North Carolina. Each Monday his teachers pick one person to be the "class leader" for the day. I only became aware of this because one sunny afternoon Ian came bounding up the stairs proclaiming, "Guess what, Daddy—I got to be the class leader today!"

Being the class leader would be a big deal for any five-year-old kid. For Ian, who is used to playing second fiddle to his older twin brother and sister, Alex and Bina, being selected as the first fiddle was even more special. Ian's exuberance caught my attention.

"Really? Class leader? That's a big deal, little buddy. What did you get to do as the class leader?"

Ian's answer was simple, funny, and in its own way, profound.

"I got to open doors for people!"

In a matter of 15 seconds, with seven simple words, Ian clarified what's most important about leadership.

How Leaders Serve Up Opportunities

I'm one of those people who can get all knotted up by over-thinking simple ideas. I love it when wise people like my five-year-old son can cut straight to what matters most. Ian is right: to be a leader is to open doors for others. Leaders open doors of perception, possibility, and most importantly, opportunity. This book is about how leaders help people and organizations by creating opportunities for growth. It is about the responsibility that leaders have for noticing, identifying, and creating opportunities for the benefit of people, organizations, and society. I call it open-door leadership.

We Complexify Leadership

In his role as class leader, Ian quickly learned an essential lesson about leadership. Opening doors is pretty much what matters most about leading people. Yet leadership, as a topic, has become increasingly complex and overwhelming. It is the most overanalyzed, thoroughly dissected, and utterly confused topic in business. In addition to umpteen thousands of books on the subject, there are leadership blogs, seminars, webinars, and retreats, all peddled by leadership gurus and consultants. I know. I am one of them.

For more than half my life, I have studied leadership. I began because in one of my earlier jobs I discovered that I was a lousy leader. One of my employees told me so . . . after threatening to quit because of my dictatorial behavior. But more on that later.

After discovering how pathetically bad I was as a leader, I started reading books on leadership and management. I got better as a leader. As a result, I decided to go to graduate school and I did my thesis on leadership.

And that's when it started. That's when I became an official contributor to the complexification of leadership. My thesis assessed—take a deep breath—*the efficacy of the initiation of psychological structure through the use of directive leadership styles as a negative correlate of role ambiguity and positive correlate of employee satisfaction in workplaces that have undergone a recent reduction in force.*

Whew!

Since graduate school two decades ago, my contributions to the complexification of leadership have only gotten more pronounced. I worked for two small leadership and team-building companies. Later, I was an executive in the change management and human performance practice at Accenture, one of the world's largest consulting firms. I eventually became the company's first full-time internal executive coach. Building on those experiences, in 2002 I founded my own management consulting company (Giant Leap Consulting) and have since designed, developed, and delivered leadership workshops for thousands of employees in prominent organizations throughout the world. I've authored a comprehensive off-the-shelf leadership-facilitator training program and two not-so-simple books.

I became a senior officer in the legion of consultants who make their livelihood by plumbing, parsing, and peddling leadership. I can complexify with the best of them. The more my consulting compatriots and I complexify leadership by using fancy-pants words and nitpicking the life out of the subject, the more we can charge you for our specialized leadership hocus-pocus. Sure, most of us are well intentioned, but by overanalyzing the subject, we've muddled up the concept of leadership.

We leadership experts, sadly, have made it harder for people to be leaders. As the checklist for what it takes to be a leader gets longer, more idealized, and more complicated, the expectations that we hold leaders to keep shifting, causing people to opt out of the chance to lead. The standards of what it means to be a leader have been raised beyond people's reach. The expectations that leaders are held to have become so inflated that practically no one can categorically qualify as a "leader" anymore. We expect leaders to be bold *and* calculated, passionate *and* reasonable, rational *and* emotional, confident *and* humble, driven *and* patient, strategic *and* tactical, competitive *and* cooperative, principled *and* flexible. Of course, it is possible to be all of those things . . . if you're God!

I Resign From the Legion of Leadership Complexifiers

This book represents my full resignation from the ranks of the Legion of Leadership Complexifiers (LLC). I pledge to you that I will speak plainly and simply. Too many books, including my earlier ones, are too dense and bloated with big SAT words, fancy quadrant models, and research citations from obscure academic journals. It's all part of the complexification business. But after a quarter of a century as a ranking member of the LLC, this complexification stuff bores and exhausts me. The density weighs me down. I suspect it weighs you down too. Reading a book shouldn't exhaust you like a long day at work.

My resignation is driven by a few changes in my own life. First, I'm older and, frankly, less insecure. When I was in my 20s, 30s, and 40s, proving how smart I was took up a lot of my time. Now that I'm in my 50s, I am more interested in having ideas connect with you than validating my intellect.

Second, having led hundreds of client engagements throughout my career and having spoken to thousands of people across the world, I've come to realize that the ideas that get through to people are those that are easiest to understand. Simple ideas are self-evident and effective. Most importantly, simple ideas get used.

The third change driving my resignation from the LLC ranks is that I'm the father of three children. They have taught me that we career-minded grown-ups are often just too smart for our own good, which is dumb. We're better off thinking about leadership with the clarity and simplicity of a five-year-old child. When I want my kids to get something done, like a house chore, I don't talk about the "strategic value-added proposition of goal attainment"; I talk about the opportunity they'll create by getting the work done. *Yes*, kids, you *can* have ice cream . . . right after you clean up your room. Simple, not complex!

We Can Simplify Leadership

Faced with a growing and ever-changing list of leadership criteria, who could possibly be successful as a leader, much less want to be one? Maybe it's time to lighten the leadership load a little. Maybe it's time to get back to the basic idea that leaders are simply creators of opportunity for others: they open doors. I wrote this book to bring leadership back to that simple idea.

Open-door leadership is a simple concept that you can quickly grasp and enjoy putting into practice. My hope is that the concepts make it appealing for you to opt in to the chance to lead. If you are in a position to open doors for people by creating opportunities that help them grow, you are a leader. This book will be especially useful if you are:

- new to the leadership ranks
- a seasoned executive, but feeling uninspired in your leadership role
- frustrated by the apathy and lack of motivation shown by your direct reports
- at the "give back" stage in your career, where helping others succeed is especially gratifying
- confused about the topic of leadership (maybe because of the glut of bloated leadership books!)
- wanting to be a better and more effective leader.

The aim of this book is simple: to inspire you to open doors of opportunity for the people you lead.

How This Book Opens Doors for You

As you read *Leaders Open Doors* you will be introduced to six unique doors of opportunity. The book is divided into two parts: "Before the Door" and "Doors of Opportunity." The first three chapters, part I, will ground you in the book's foundational concepts; part II covers six chapters, each describing a unique opportunity door. *Leaders Open Doors* is meant to be a fast and useful read. It is also designed to help you take immediate action. At the end of each chapter you'll be provided with some specific actions and reflection questions to provide momentum toward strengthening your open-door leadership.

Chapter	You'll Learn	Key Takeaways
Preface	What a leader is	❖ Leadership should be simple, not complex. ❖ A leader creates opportunities for others.
Chapter 1: Introducing Open-Door Leadership	Why leadership means opening doors	❖ Open-door leaders have four key skills.
Chapter 2: Opportunity Focus	Why focusing on problem solving is far less effective than focusing on the opportunities those "problems" nearly always provide	❖ Leaders fill people with courage. ❖ Pull through opportunity; don't push through fear. ❖ Sharpen your own opportunity-focus.

Chapter	You'll Learn	Key Takeaways
Chapter 3: Purposeful Discomfort	Why making people uncomfortable—in a way they can absorb—is every leader's primary job	❖ Create discomfort for both yourself and others to inspire them to grow.
Chapter 4: The Proving-Ground Door	Why giving people opportunities to prove themselves taps into their need to excel and can supercharge motivation	❖ Design gradual proving-ground opportunities to help people grow. ❖ Refine your own skills as an open-door leader.
Chapter 5: The Thought-Shifting Door	How the actions leaders take can help broaden and shift someone's perspective so he can face challenges more creatively	❖ Disrupting mental routines encourages creativity. ❖ Symbols encourage thought shift. ❖ Small language changes can change perception.
Chapter 6: The Door to a Second Chance	How you can gain deep loyalty and commitment when you open a door to a second chance, especially after big mistakes	❖ Transform mistakes into platforms for growth. ❖ Strategic forgiveness can engender loyalty and growth.
Chapter 7: Opening Doors for Others	Why leaders need to pay special attention to the needs of people who are outside the majority	❖ Break through "tribal" thinking and include Others in your organization.

Chapter	You'll Learn	Key Takeaways
Chapter 8: The Door to Personal Transformation	How instrumental leaders can be in bringing about career and life transformations for people	❖ Leaders should model transformation first. ❖ Open-door leaders intentionally help others transform. ❖ Open-door leaders promote accountability. ❖ Effective feedback is both diplomatic and honest.
Chapter 9: The Door to Your Open Heart	How you can have the greatest positive impact on people only when you open yourself up and show your true self to those you lead	❖ Caring affects loyalty and performance. ❖ Opening up about who you really are can strengthen your bond with those you lead—and why you should do it.

A Word Before You Start

The approach to leadership described in this book is based on the simple and well-tested idea that leaders help people and organizations grow when they focus on creating opportunities for others. But just because the idea is simple doesn't mean it is easy. Open-door leadership takes work. So let's get started. How do you start opening doors for people, and what's in it for you if you do? Turn to the first part to find out.

Part I

Before the Door

Being an open-door leader requires understanding what an open-door leader does. It also means having an opportunity mind-set, a significant shift from the more common threat-focused way of leading. Many leaders hyperfocus on mitigating risk, viewing most situations as threats or problems. But when leaders view situations as risks, threats, or problems, they inject fear and anxiety into people, generating pessimism. In the long run, fear damages morale and performance.

Open-door leaders view challenging situations as opportunities, not problems. Instead of injecting people with fear, they help people see the opportunities that the challenges provide, inspiring them with excitement and hope. The resulting optimism lifts morale and performance.

In this part you'll discover:

- the four skills of an open-door leader
- why your approach to opportunity matters

- why using fear to motivate people makes for lousy leadership
- why making people uncomfortable is one of an open-door leader's most important jobs.

Chapter 1

Introducing Open-Door Leadership

All that is valuable in human society depends upon the opportunity for development accorded the individual.
—Albert Einstein

Leadership is often defined as a set of behaviors by which one person influences others toward the achievement of goals. Put more simply, leadership is about momentum and results. While these definitions are true, they somehow fall short. What mechanism should a leader use, for example, to "influence" strong performance? Has leadership evolved beyond carrots and sticks? And what about the people being led? Besides a paycheck, what do they get out of getting results for the leader? What's in it for them? After all, the leader's success depends on them, right?

What's missing is *opportunity*. In exchange for advancing the leader's goals, the people being led should expect work opportunities that provide for:

- growth and personal development
- career fulfillment and enrichment
- acquisition of new skills
- financial gain and other rewards
- greater access to leadership roles.

People and organizations grow and develop to the extent that they capitalize on opportunities to do so. Opportunities are important to leaders because they're important to the people they lead. Opportunities are the venues where people can try, test, better, and even find themselves. The leader's job is to match the opportunity to the person and to help the person—and the organization—exploit that opportunity for all it's worth. Open-door leadership is about noticing, identifying, and creating opportunities for those being led.

Think for a moment about a leader you greatly admire. Pick someone who has led you, rather than someone on the world stage. What do you admire about him or her? Did he open a door to an opportunity where you could grow your skills or improve yourself, such as asking you to lead a high-profile project? Did she help illuminate a blind spot by giving you candid feedback that caused you to see yourself in a different and more honest way? Did he build your confidence by asking for your perspective, input, and ideas? Or did she openly advocate for your promotion, showing you how much she valued you? What doors did he open for you?

My bet is that the leaders you most admire are the ones who left you better off than they found you by creating opportunities that helped you grow. How?

- by being open *to* you, valuing your input and perspective

- by being open *with* you, telling you the truth even if the truth is difficult to hear

- by helping you be receptive to new possibilities and experiences and new ways of perceiving and thinking.

Open-door leadership involves creating or assigning opportunities in order to promote growth. By promoting the growth of those they lead, leaders increase the likelihood of their own success and advancement. They also increase the likelihood of creating other leaders, which is essential to building a lasting leadership legacy. Leaders create leaders by opening doors of opportunity that have a positive and lasting impact on the behavior of those they lead.

"Open Door" Is Not a Policy!

To be clear, open-door leadership is not about having an open-door policy. Such policies are just more management hokum. One of the surest signs of a rookie leader is the claim, "I have an open-door policy, and my door is always open so my employees can get to me." Allowing yourself to be continuously interrupted is a recipe for lousy leadership. If your door is always open, how on earth can you get any work done on behalf of the people who are interrupting you? Open-door leadership is not about having a policy of keeping your door open *to* others. It's about taking actions to open doors *for* others. It is about so much more than giving people unfettered access to you.

I Knew an Open-Door Leader

After having spoken with thousands of executives over the course of two decades, I am convinced that career advancement is nearly always a function of the presence, influence, and support of a dedicated open-door leader. They always seem to appear when we need them, nudging us along, encouraging our growth, and helping us see and move toward our potential.

Let me share a very personal story about one such leader's profound impact on my life and career. The story helps illustrates the concept of open-door leadership and introduces the four skills that open-door leaders possess.

I used to drink too much. Way too much. I drank to the point where my drinking started interfering with my life and relationships. Eventually I entered a recovery program and got help. Life got better.

Three years after getting sober and attending lots of support group meetings, I decided to reveal to my boss, Hines Brannan, a partner at Accenture, that I was in recovery. After working for him for three years, I wanted him to know me beyond the person he knew me to be at work.

Keep in mind that Accenture is not some young, urban start-up company with a foosball table in the break room. It is one of the world's largest management and technology consulting firms. The culture is, at once, professional, disciplined, ambitious, and . . . stiff. While I didn't expect my boss to pat me on my shoulder and say, "Good for you. You're a drunk!" I expected more of a reaction than I got. After I told him that I was in recovery, Hines looked at me quizzically, and muttered, "I see." Then he made some small-talk comments and hurried on to another meeting.

I regretted having told him and wondered whether I had just damaged my career.

Then, about two weeks later, Hines called me into his office and said, "I've been thinking about what you told me a few weeks ago. What I didn't tell you then is that I am the chairman of the board of directors of a nonprofit agency called the Georgia Council on Substance Abuse. It's based here in Atlanta. Accenture recently agreed to do a pro bono research project, and we're going to be providing them with a small team to do the research. I'd like for you to lead the project. Remember, I'm the board chair, so I'm going to be here with you every step of the way."

Door open.

My boss had created an opportunity for me to align my career goals and my personal interests with Accenture's goals in serving the client.

It was the first time as a new manager that I got to lead my own project team. Given my personal experience with substance abuse, you can imagine how much passion I had for the work. With that passion, and the support of my boss, I did a great job. Because I did a great job, new doors opened and I got other meaningful projects.

There are a number of factors at play in this story. First, to open a door for me, Hines had to have a fuller knowledge of my background than just my current skills. He had to know what I wanted to achieve with my career and the contribution I was hoping to make. He also had to know something about my outside-of-work identity. Second, he had to make the connection between an opportunity that existed and my *suitedness* to take advantage of it. Third, he had to have a clear vision about how the opportunity could benefit the company and me. The opportunity would need to deepen my experience and increase my skills, making me a more valuable employee. Fourth, he had to have a genuine interest in seeing me succeed. In short, he had to care about me.

Using this story as an example, we can draw out the four skills that open-door leaders commonly apply. You need to:

- **Know your employees:** Have extensive knowledge about the backgrounds, needs, and desires of your employees. Invest time in getting to know them beyond the tasks they get done for you. Ask them directly about their career goals and aspirations— what do they want to get out of this job? Keep in mind the goal isn't to intrude or interrogate. It's to gain insight into their goals, strengths, and motivations. We'll talk more about this in the coming chapters.

- **Match suitedness:** Draw connections between the opportunity and the developmental needs of your employees. This involves constantly being on the look-out for opportunities that can advance your employee's career. Then, when opportunities are identified ask yourself, "Whose growth and development would pursuing this opportunity most advance?"

- **Envision the desired results:** Have a clear picture of the desired benefits that given opportunities present for the employees and the organization. Once an opportunity is assigned, do some "future-casting" with your employee, thinking through the potential benefits—to the employee and the organization—that could emerge if the opportunity is successfully accomplished. Also give some thought to the actions that will have to occur to maximize the probability of success.

- **Provide ongoing support:** Genuinely want, and support, your employees' success. This skill is an outgrowth of the other three. When you really know the aims of your employees—when you've assigned them to a juicy opportunity that's ripe for their skills and worked with them to develop a clear picture of a successful outcome—you almost can't help but take a strong interest in their success. Stay involved by periodically asking what support they need from you, removing barriers that might block their progress, and offering encouragement and guidance when they hit roadblocks and bottlenecks.

The more you cultivate these skills, the more you will see opportunities to open doors for others. The starting place is a strong opportunity focus, which is the subject of the next chapter.

Open-Door Actions and Reflections

1. Think back over the course of your career.

   • What are some opportunities that have been given to you?

2. How have those opportunities helped you grow personally and professionally?

   • Which opportunity stands out as particularly important?

   • Who brought the opportunity to you?

   • What is your impression of him or her as a leader?

   • Why do you think you were selected for the opportunity instead of someone else?

3. Look over the four skills of an open-door leader.

   • Which ones did the person who brought you the opportunity use?

   • Based on what you've read so far about open-door leadership, was the person who brought you the opportunity an open-door leader?

Chapter 2

Opportunity Focus

*Opportunity is more powerful even than
conquerors and prophets.*
—**Benjamin Disraeli**

===

Do you aim to be a problem-focused leader or an opportunity-focused leader?

Many work environments place a premium on leaders with critical-thinking and problem-solving skills. However, that premium often places too much emphasis on being *critical* and dealing with *problems*. In such workplaces, leaders can become downers, always harping on what's wrong and what needs to be fixed. Such leaders often resort to stoking people's fears to motivate them to get things done. This fear-stoking is exemplified by one of the most overused phrases in the history of business: *What keeps me awake at night is . . .*

Think about it. When leaders talk about (or more often brag about) what keeps them awake at night, aren't they really just showcasing their fears and anxieties? It's as if some leaders believe that the only way they'll get any rest is to make the entire workforce share in their fears. Unless people are as afraid as they are, the leaders think that no one will be motivated enough to address whatever is causing them to lose sleep. But putting people on the your 24-hour fear cycle isn't motivating at all—insomnia shouldn't be a leadership badge of honor.

Leaders would be better served to talk about what gets them up in the morning instead of what keeps them awake at night. Opportunity attracts and excites employees more than problems do. People want to follow leaders who have such confidence in them and the opportunities that the future holds. People want to follow leaders who sleep soundly at night.

Are You a Spiller or a Filler?

Leaders generally fall into two broad categories: *spillers* and *fillers*. Spillers motivate people by stoking their fears. They view most situations as threats to be controlled and neutralized. When confronting a challenging situation, they immediately jump to the worst possible potential outcomes. By injecting you with fear and anxiety, they drain off your confidence and courage—hence the term "spiller." Always expecting a catastrophe, spillers blow things way out of proportion. They say things like:

- You have a huge problem on your hands.

- Do you realize how much that puts us at risk?
- If you mess up, we'll all be in trouble.
- Do not, I repeat, *do not* make a mistake.

Fillers, conversely, motivate people by appealing to their innate desire to excel. Instead of playing not to lose, as spillers do, fillers play to win. In the same situation, they look for opportunities to exploit, not threats to control. Instead of transmitting fear and anxiety, they give followers a fuller sense of confidence and excitement. They say things like:

- Hmm, this is a challenging situation . . . and it's full of opportunity.
- Here's why I think you're the right person to take on this challenge and why it would be good for your career growth.
- I have every confidence that you'll be successful, and here's the support you can expect from me . . .
- What do *you* think? What should our first steps be?

Keep in mind that both fillers and spillers can get a good job out of you. You may perform well for spillers because you know how much trouble you'll get into if you don't. You'll perform well for fillers because they believe in you and you don't want to let them down. However there is one consequential difference between working for a spiller and working for a filler—fillers get deep loyalty from the people they lead; spillers get deep resentment.

Open-Door Leader Examples

Opportunities come in many forms. Sometimes they simply present themselves at an opportune moment. Other times they are intentionally created by the open-door leader. Here are some real-life examples:

The owner of a respected construction company notices that one of the company's mid-level managers seems particularly skilled at building client relationships and winning work. He is also aware that there is no successor to the company's VP of business development, who is a few years away from retirement. He reassigns the manager to work directly with the VP, with an eye toward his eventually becoming the VP's successor. The owner has the opportunity to fill a position with a qualified person, and the manager has the opportunity to grow into a position where he can excel.

The managing director of a large consulting firm tasks a new manager with facilitating the director's weekly staff meeting while he's on a two-week overseas business trip. Every meeting attendee, including his former boss, is more senior than the manager. The managing director knew that the manager was looking for more opportunities to demonstrate leadership and he decided that facilitating a dominating group of senior execs would be a great start.

The executive committee of a $300 million company decides to mobilize a small "Lessons Learned" team of emerging leaders to conduct postmortems on large successful and unsuccessful projects. The team members were chosen based on the skills that the organization needs them to grow, not the skills that they currently have. The team is responsible for gathering lessons and best practices and making recommendations to the executive committee.

During the early parts of a three-day strategic-planning off-site meeting, the senior executive team of a medical device company receives a call from the home office confirming that the FDA is recommending a recall of one of their products. Instead of cancelling the off-site meeting, the execs decide that the emergency presents an opportunity for their successors—who are still in the home office—to lead the company through a substantial challenge. The execs make themselves available for morning and evening conference calls to stay apprised and lend support and direction.

Why Leading Through Fear Is Cheap Leadership

If you're a parent, you know that using threats is an effective way of getting your children to do what you want them to do. Whether you're threatening to remove something your kids want or threatening to punish them for some naughty thing they're doing, fear works. I know. I've used it myself, even on my sweet five-year-old son, Ian. When he was going through his terrible twos and being disobedient, I would threaten to put on a Halloween mask that scared him to get him to be good. "Ian!" I'd bark. "Stop that right now or I'm going to put on the mask!" Although the Department of Social Services may not have approved of my scare tactics, they worked. All it took for me to quickly shift Ian from naughty to nice was the simple threat of a scary face.

Using fear to motivate people is cheap leadership. Any two-bit dictator can use fear to get things done. It takes no finesse or intelligence and ultimately works against the leader. The temporary spike in motivation from stoking people's fears is offset by the long-term impacts of deep resentment, performance-draining anxiety, and ill will. More evolved and thoughtful leaders choose to pull people toward the behaviors they want, instead of pushing them away from the behaviors they don't want. For example, my wife uses a compliment system to promote good behavior with our kids. Each time one of them finishes a chore they get to put a small stone (a "compliment") in a jar that's been set aside just for them. Then, when they've gathered enough stones they get a small reward, like dinner at Chuck E. Cheese.

If you want workers to act like adults, you have to lead like an adult. Instead of constantly drawing their attention to the bad things that will happen if they mess up, work with them to identify the actions and priorities that will increase their likelihood of succeeding. Remind them that taking on challenges is how leaders earn their merit badges at work. Be sure to specify what rewards they can expect if they succeed—including the chance to be involved in more opportunities. Pulling people toward good behavior instead of threatening them out of bad behavior is a healthier and more mature way of leading.

Opportunity Attracts

Fear and excitement prompt the same neurological responses. Think for a moment about what happens to you, physiologically, when you are really, really afraid. Your heart races, your palms sweat, your breath gets faster and shorter, and your stomach teems with butterflies. Well, guess what? Those same physiological responses happen when you are going to have sex!

Fear and excitement are both high arousal states. Although there are almost no neurological or physiological differences, there is one critical distinction between the conditions of fear and excitement—you experience fear as displeasure and excitement as pleasure. Thus you move toward situations that provide pleasure and avoid situations that provoke displeasure. By viewing and explaining situations as opportunities, you create a field of excitement where employees are more apt to face challenges than shirk them.

Focusing on opportunity instead of problems is not just a matter of semantics. The following are some specific impacts of keeping an opportunity focus.

Opportunity pulls.

Leading by stoking people's fears provokes anxiety and negative thoughts of impending painful consequences. Opportunities, on the other hand, are hopeful situations that evoke positive thoughts of pleasurable rewards. Leadership is most effective when it moves people toward a desired outcome, rather than getting them to run away from a bad outcome. Opportunity attracts; fear repels.

Opportunity points in the right direction.

When you are talking about opportunities, you are talking about the conditions you want, instead of the conditions you want to prevent from happening. Because outcomes often follow the direction of our thoughts, it's best to focus on what you want. Saying, "Our opportunity is to keep the ball in the air," is better than "Whatever you do, don't drop that ball!"

Opportunity activates imagination.

We "take advantage of" or "capitalize on" opportunities. They are conditions that don't yet exist and require people's hard work and imagination to be fully exploited.

Opportunity inspires courage.

Opportunities are not "sure things" and the positive outcome you hope to create is not guaranteed. Thus, opportunities come with potential risks. The risk is what infuses the pursuit of opportunities with excitement.

Opportunity begets opportunity.

Wouldn't you rather have your employees coming to you with new ideas and opportunities they want you to support, instead of problems they want you to resolve? When you model opportunistic thinking, you increase the likelihood of building a self-sufficient, "can do" spirit among employees.

Of Big "O"s and Little "o"s

Capitalizing on a really big opportunity often requires marshaling a host of smaller opportunities across an organization. In these instances, the open-door leader's job is to broaden the opportunity landscape for the entire organization. To illustrate this concept, let's consider the story of Sutton Bacon.

To the surprise of many, Sutton became the president and CEO of the Nantahala Outdoor Center (NOC) in his late 20s. People wondered how a guy so young could be given the opportunity to lead a whitewater-adventure facility with such a rich history. But the choice made sense. Despite his age, Sutton was perfectly suited for the job—he had previously been the president of American Whitewater and had worked as a marketing strategy consultant after graduating from Emory University. What mattered more was how deeply Sutton loved the NOC. He had learned to kayak there when he was five years old. He knew, and valued, the NOC's rich history. He also knew of its financial struggles and competitive threats—like the new year-round whitewater facility that had just opened up in Charlotte, North Carolina, only two hours down the road. Sutton, part kayaker and part hard-core business consultant, convinced the NOC's board of directors that he was the right guy for the job.

The big opportunity was to create long-term sustainability for the NOC, which would require solidifying the NOC's preeminence as a whitewater mecca while expanding its offerings. The challenge for Sutton and his team was to get the bulk of the workforce—raft guides—to see that the NOC's opportunities would be limited if it continued thinking of itself as just a rafting business. Sutton felt that turning the NOC into an adventure business would create far more opportunities for everyone. More customers could be served, more money could be made, and more fun could be had if the NOC transformed from a rafting outfitter to a provider of memorable *adventure experiences*.

Becoming a world-leading provider of adventure experiences would require changing or reinvigorating nearly every aspect of the NOC. Sutton and his management team aimed at the larger opportunity (sustainability) by creating many smaller opportunities. They started hosting more national and international canoeing and kayaking competitions, which brought more exposure to the NOC and more revenue to fund other ideas. They launched more informal events, too, like the annual Halloween Pumpkin Run, where kayakers competed by scooping up bobbing pumpkins on their way down the rapids. They opened Slow Joe's Café, a small sandwich shop right at the river's edge. They even successfully convinced the leaders in Bryson City, North Carolina, to lift the NOC's alcohol license restrictions. People could now buy beer and wine from the NOC instead of bringing it in their coolers.

As Sutton and his team created more opportunities, more money was generated, allowing them to create even more opportunities. They started an instant-photo business that let families purchase high-quality photos of themselves immediately after storming down the river. They opened an outdoor store in downtown Gatlinburg, Tennessee, as well as a LEED-certified retail store in the historic Grove Park Inn in Asheville, North Carolina.

Most importantly, Sutton and his team significantly increased the number and types of adventure programs available to customers. In addition to whitewater rafting and kayaking, patrons could now go zip-lining, on jet boat rides, mountain biking, high-ropes excursions, fly fishing, and international adventure excursions. The NOC was now squarely in the business of adventure.

Sutton and his team of open-door leaders broadened the NOC's opportunity landscape. They shifted people's view of the NOC from a North Carolina summertime rafting outfitter to a vibrant world-class commercial business enterprise offering unique adventure experiences. By tightly marrying thrilling adventure and sound business practices, the NOC was becoming sustainable. Sutton even testified before the U.S. House of Representatives Small Business Committee, where he was honored as a "Hero of Small Business."

In the process of broadening the NOC's overall opportunity landscape, Sutton himself became an open-door leader. None of the opportunities his company expanded into could have been accomplished without Sutton opening the doors for his team to try new ideas and grow into new positions.

Bear in mind that the opportunities Sutton and his team created weren't without hardship. Some of the NOC's most tenured personnel fiercely resisted the changes. They felt like the balance had swung too far toward capitalism and too far away from the communal culture they had worked so hard to create. A few people left. A few were asked to leave.

Opportunities bring about change, and change often comes with turbulence. Some people may find changes threatening and disruptive and thus struggle to embrace them. Open-door leaders have to be patient, keeping the end game in mind. People need time to catch on to the potential that the opportunities hold.

The most satisfying opportunities are those that benefit customers and employees. Sutton and his team wanted to make sure that the staff directly benefitted from the changes, so they lobbied for, and were granted, limited access to the Cheoah River, a scenic class IV and V river. Now the staff could paddle in a remote and unspoiled river that had been closed off to kayakers for years. The team also created new play holes on the Nantahala River, which were irresistible fun for the kayaking enthusiasts among the staff. Finally, they added Wi-Fi throughout the NOC's Bryson City outpost so staff and customers could access the Internet. Soon, people started to "get it." The best days of the NOC were in front of it, not behind it.

Eventually all the opportunities, big and small, helped transform the NOC and its culture. Many of the NOC's staff took pride in knowing that they had helped their organization become the largest outdoor recreation company in the United States, offering more than 120 different adventure programs in 10 states and serving up to a million visitors annually. The *New York Times* recognized the NOC as the nation's premier paddling school, *Outside Magazine* called it the best place to learn how to paddle, and *National Geographic Adventure Magazine* declared it one of the best outfitters on earth.

Open-Door Leaders Are Opportunity Creators

A leader's primary job is to actively create opportunities that bring about real and concrete benefits. A leader should leave us better off than they found us. Open-door leaders don't sell hope. In fact they don't *sell* anything. They *build*.

They experiment. They act. They create. And like Sutton and his team, by relentlessly focusing on creating opportunities for customers and employees, they open lots and lots of doors.

Open-Door Actions and Reflections

1. Write down your answers to these questions:

   - What are some work-related opportunities or goals that "get you up in the morning"?

   - In your work, what are you most excited about right now? Increase the time you spend doing things that awaken your spirit at work!

2. Identify one work-related "problem" that is currently causing you anxiety. List the specific opportunities that this challenge presents. From now on, whenever you speak about this work challenge, refer to it as an opportunity.

3. Identify one leader you've worked with and admire. Using the continuum on the next page, place an "X" on the spot that best reflects the focus of the leader. Resist the temptation to say it depends on the situation. Just think in general terms.

4. Now think of a leader with whom you've worked that you least admire. Use the same continuum to mark their spot.

5. Now consider your focus. Where do you fit on the continuum?

problem-focus						opportunity-focus			
1	2	3	4	5	6	7	8	9	10

The leader you most admire likely has more of an opportunity focus than the leader you least admire. If you want to be admired too, you'll focus on raising your opportunity-focus number. Do that by reaching out to the admired leader for mentoring. Ask:

- When you come up against a challenging situation, what are your first thoughts?

- In your career, who influenced you to view challenges as opportunities?

- What advice can you give for helping me see the opportunities that challenging situations present?

Chapter 3

Purposeful Discomfort

*Move out of your comfort zone. You can only
grow if you are willing to feel awkward and
uncomfortable when you try something new.*
—Brian Tracy

═══════════════════════════════════════

As creators of opportunity, open-door leaders are also
providers of purposeful discomfort. Why? Virginia Rometty,
CEO of IBM, had it right when she said, "Growth and comfort
do not coexist," at *Fortune* magazine's Most Powerful Women
Summit. We grow, develop, and progress by pursuing opportunities that put us outside our comfort zone. Opportunities
create discomfort.

The trick is that you have to provide uncomfortable
opportunities that provoke growth, not set people up for
failure. As a leader, you have to provide tasks or situations
that are enough of a stretch that they motivate people to
move outside their comfort zones, but not so far outside
that they debilitate performance. While some level of fear

and anxiety is natural, and perhaps even necessary, too much is demoralizing and can cause people to stew with resentment (see the previous chapter).

By nudging people into discomfort, you help activate their courage, which is what they need to face the fear that discomfort provokes. Consider, for example, some of these common uncomfortable work situations and the opportunities they present to demonstrate courage:

- giving a presentation to your boss's boss
- taking a job with demands that eclipse your current skills
- delegating a risky task to a new or untested employee
- enforcing new performance standards on employees who are longer tenured than you
- admitting to a client or customer that you or your company made a big mistake.

It may surprise you that your job as an open-door leader is to make people uncomfortable, but good opportunities create discomfort. When you are asked to lead a group of employees for the very first time, that is an opportunity. It's also uncomfortable. When you are asked to make a new product pitch to the board of directors, that is an opportunity. It is also uncomfortable. When you are slotted to be your boss's successor, that is an opportunity. It's also uncomfortable. If something is uncomfortable, there's a good chance that it presents an opportunity to grow.

Deliver Discomfort in Doses

A large Chicago-based construction company uses purposeful discomfort as a key feature of its leadership-succession program. The bimonthly leadership workshops start by having each of the 25 up-and-coming leaders give a two-minute presentation that is focused on the progress they've made using the leadership concepts they were introduced to during the previous workshops. Keep in mind that the presentations are videotaped and given in front of the company's most senior executives, including the CEO. Getting them out of their comfort zones serves two purposes:

- It holds them accountable to actually implementing the program concepts.

- It forces them to deal with the discomfort that so often comes with giving a presentation.

When you watch the participants' videotapes you can see the arc of their progress. The confidence that these leaders gain in giving presentations during the course of the 18-month program is nothing short of amazing. Early on, many of them are like awkward teenagers, stumbling through their two minutes, hemming and hawing and umming. Plenty of them suffer from an all-out brain freeze, abruptly stopping, not knowing what to say next. But by the last workshop, everyone is able to stand and speak with confidence and poise. They've grown because they did something uncomfortable. As the program progresses, they become more comfortable with discomfort.

You have to be able to present confidently if you want people to believe in the direction you set as their leader. So if you're in a leadership-development program with the aim of becoming a more confident and influential leader, you'd better learn how to present. That requires stepping straight into your discomfort zone. And if you're leading the aspiring leaders, your job is to create the opportunity for them to experience this discomfort.

Create Safe Discomfort

Getting people to do purposefully uncomfortable things is easier if you also create a safe environment for them. They have to know that you have their back, that the discomfort won't be permanent, and that it's truly purposeful. Otherwise, they'll think that you're a mad scientist and they're guinea pigs in some diabolical experiment. For example, before the high-potential leaders started giving the two-minute presentations, the CEO explained how presenting was connected to the concept of leadership, that it was fully expected that they'd make lots of mistakes, and that they should seek progress, not perfection. The CEO, whom everyone admired for being a great communicator, also let people know that he started out as a terrible public speaker but forced himself to improve by taking advantage of every opportunity he could find to speak publicly.

Some semblance of psychological safety is important. The idea is not to get people to do *wildly* uncomfortable things, just *willfully* uncomfortable things. They need to know that you're asking them to do uncomfortable things to promote their growth and career advancement. To make this work, you need to know your employees' goals, aspirations, and areas for growth, and then provide uncomfortable opportunities that promote those aims. For example, if you've got a painfully introverted worker who also aspires to be a leader, you might have that person lead the weekly status meeting in your absence. Conversely, if you've got an employee who's extraverted to the point of being offensive or oblivious about how everyone else perceives him, you might have him be the note taker at the same meeting, instructing the über-extravert not to talk, only to listen and scribe. The opportunities you provide as a leader should be outside those areas where people already feel comfortably skilled.

Role Model: Seek Discomfort Yourself

People will also be much more willing to move toward discomfort if they see you doing uncomfortable things too. When asked to comment on how risk taking had influenced his career, the division president of a large communications company put it this way: "Throughout my career, I've always been willing to take jobs that were outside my skill set. Some people think that's crazy, but I'm telling you that I wouldn't be sitting here as president if I had done it any other way. It's dangerous to be too safe. Look, even today I'm outside my comfort zone. I'm an engineer, but

I'm basically leading a sales organization. I knew next to nothing about sales before I took this job. Getting out of my comfort zone keeps me challenged. I want our people to do the same thing. They need to scrape their knees like I did, but know that I won't let them break their legs."

It's easier to get people to do uncomfortable things when you lead the way. There is no more powerful influencer of behavior in the workplace than the role modeling of the leaders. To this end, ask yourself, "What is the most uncomfortable thing I've done at work in the last three months?" If you don't have a solid answer, maybe you're too comfortable. Here are some examples of minimally uncomfortable actions you can take to role model purposeful discomfort:

- Request to cover an agenda item at your boss's next status meeting.

- Make an apology to someone whose development you feel like you've been neglecting.

- Go to night school and take a certification class that's relevant to your job.

- Purposely solicit anonymous feedback about your leadership style and effectiveness by going through a 360-degree leadership-feedback process.

Open-Door Actions and Reflections

1. Use the boxes below to compare your answers to these two questions:

   - Where are you playing it too safe in your career?

   - What cost is too much safety is having on your career?

Playing It Safe	Cost to Career

2. Now that you know where you're playing it too safe and what it's costing you, identify two or three specific courageous actions you could take to move into discomfort. Mark where on the comfort/ discomfort continuum each action resides. Actions with a rating of five or less may not be courageous— or uncomfortable—enough!

comfort   discomfort

| 1 | 2 | 3 | 4 | 5 | 6 | 7 | 8 | 9 | 10 |

3. Consider the degree of comfort your direct reports have in executing their job assignments. For each direct report, identify one purposefully uncomfortable skill-stretching task.

Part II

Doors of Opportunity

The chapters in the first part were about establishing an open-door leader mindset. Leaders are most effective when they elevate people to a higher standard of performance by opening many doors of opportunity. Adopting an opportunity focus means viewing challenges as things to be expected, valued, and embraced. However, moving others toward opportunity also means purposefully nudging them out of their comfort zones. Opportunities are uncomfortable things, and open-door leaders help people and organizations grow to the extent that they inspire them to do the uncomfortable.

This section builds upon the foundational principles covered in part I and introduces six unique doors that any aspiring open-door leader needs to know how to open.

In this part you'll learn:

- why giving people something to prove is powerfully important

- how open-door leadership often involves getting people to see the world differently

- why second chances are important, and when to give them
- why tapping into the perspectives of those who stand outside the majority is critically important to your success as an open-door leader and to their success as employees
- how open-door leaders can bring about personal transformation in themselves and others
- why open-door leadership requires opening your heart to those you lead.

Chapter 4

The Proving-Ground Door

*One of the beautiful things about baseball
is that every once in a while you come into
a situation where you want to, and where you
have to, reach down and prove something.*

—Nolan Ryan

On any given afternoon between Memorial Day and Labor Day, Little League baseball games are underway at neighborhood ballparks throughout America. While there's no guarantee which team will win—be it the Johnsonville Juggernauts or the Midville Mudslingers—what is guaranteed is that at least one little bench-sitting baseball player will be pleading, "Put me in, Coach! I'm ready to play!"

Every kid who plays baseball dreams of making a big play or hitting a home run. But first they have to be given the shot, and it's the coach who decides who gets to step up to the plate.

Adults are like kids, just with bigger clothes and bigger egos. We all want a chance to shine. We want to prove—to ourselves and to others—what we can do. But our chance to shine hinges on whether we get a proving ground where we can test our mettle. Often, unless our leader opens a door to an opportunity proving ground, our skills will languish or we will go unnoticed among our teammates.

Few things are as motivating as having something to prove. It is what propels the entrepreneurial spirit that so many organizations are desperate to ignite. Open-door leaders are wise to take advantage of the deep-seated desire that human beings have to prove their worth. Often, the open-door leader is the only person with the keys to the proving-ground door.

Who Deserves an Opportunity?

Who, exactly, should the open-door leader give an opportunity to? Why everyone of course! That said, opportunities are more urgently needed for a person who is:

- early in her career and needs to prove her meddle
- late in his career and needs a "swan song" assignment
- suffering after a career setback and needs to prove herself to herself in order to reclaim her confidence
- hungry to exercise and showcase his latent skills so he can advance

- ready to jump onto the management track

- long overdue for a good opportunity, having earned the right to have her moment to shine

- slotted to succeed a beloved senior executive and in need of a substantial and visible "win" to gain loyalty

- a flight risk because he is under challenged and thirsty to add more value and take on more responsibility.

Small Proving Before Big Proving

As an open-door leader, you have to dole out opportunities in absorbable doses, otherwise you may inadvertently set someone up for failure. Often, the best way to prepare a person for a big opportunity is to give him or her a number of smaller, lead-up opportunities. In other words, little doors come before big doors.

Early in my career, I worked for an Atlanta-based team-building company called Executive Adventure (EA). I learned about the company—which provides spirited team-development services, often involving experiential activities—through an in-flight magazine article just after completing my graduate studies in organizational development. It was the kind of company any guy in his late 20s would want to join! EA's services involved putting groups of corporate execs through fun team-building obstacles in scenic outdoor locations—some of the obstacles, commonly called "ropes courses," were suspended 40 feet in the air. Particularly attractive was the fact that I wouldn't have to wear a business suit, just rugged outerwear.

I was hired into the company in a sales position. Although it wasn't the position I was hoping for, I figured it was a good way to get my foot in the door until an opportunity emerged for me to move into a facilitator position.

Bob Carr, the founder of the company and a pioneer in corporate team building, was very aware of my desire to move into the role of team-building facilitator. He knew my educational background and my career aspirations. But because I was a newcomer to the profession, he couldn't risk having me facilitate sessions for EA's high-profile clients, which included Delta Airlines, Coca-Cola, Prudential Insurance, the Home Depot, and many other renowned companies. After all, how could a young buck like me offer guidance on how to be a strong team to people who had been working on teams for many more years than I had? At the same time, I would never be able to provide such guidance if I never got the chance to work with the corporate groups. I was stuck in the proverbial need-experience-to-get-experience catch-22.

Each year, EA also did a number of projects for nonprofit organizations. While nonprofits deserved, and got, the same quality programs as our for-profit clients, working for nonprofits came with less pressure—executives working in nonprofits were less uptight than their corporate counterparts, who often exhibit aggressive and sometimes cutthroat competition. Nonprofits thrive to the extent that they build cooperative alliances with funders, policy makers, and other stakeholders. Most nonprofits are also focused on delivering programs and services (or creating opportunities) for people who are less fortunate, so they tend to be socially conscious. As a result, execs in nonprofits are generally more forgiving than their for-profit counterparts.

Knowing that the risk of upsetting a nonprofit client with a rookie facilitator was lower, Bob gave me my first shot at facilitating a group while working with a nonprofit. Like the other facilitators, I received a briefing about the goals of the event from the client. Like the other facilitators, I knew which activities we were going to do and what learning points we aimed to draw out during the facilitated discussions after each team-building activity. Unlike the other facilitators, however, I had no actual experience. Knowing this, Bob always kept within earshot of me as I worked with my assigned group.

More than 20 years later, I can still see Bob's face and his satisfied "the kid's got promise" grin. He saw potential in my unrefined skills as a facilitator. Not long after the project, he gave me another nonprofit assignment and then another and another. Eventually, I got the chance to work with for-profit corporate groups too.

All of my early work with EA became a proving ground where I could sharpen my skills and grow my confidence. So much of this had to do with the things Bob did for me as an open-door leader. He was very hands-on and would set aside time to work with me after each workshop. He would ask me to critique myself and then provide his own candid feedback. He suggested more impactful ways to word my questions. He shared stories about mistakes he had made along the way and what those mistakes taught him. Finally, he frequently pointed out the progress I was making but often couldn't see myself. All these things helped me become more confident, and they also helped Bob become more confident in me, culminating in him asking me to take over EA's largest client contract, the Ford Motor Company. The program involved conducting 27 team-building programs for Ford's New Employee Orientation program at their world headquarters in Dearborn, Michigan. I was responsible for leading a team of seven other EA facilitators and was Ford's key point of contact.

My proving ground with Ford turned out to be a true field of play. I was responsible for designing a scenario-based business-simulation activity that involved having teams of new Ford engineers build cars out of PVC pipe and then race them against each other. The work was challenging, mentally stimulating, and required the full use of my imagination. The client held me to high standards, demanded solid work, and could be "Ford Tough." The entire experience made me a better and more capable professional.

Remember, I started out at EA as a sales guy. But with the support of Bob, a hands-on, open-door leader, I received proving opportunities to grow, develop, and progress. My work with Ford remains one of the highlights of the early part of my career, which culminated with my being named vice president at Executive Adventure. Eventually, I was facilitating more EA programs than Bob. Working with Bob convinced me of the value of opening doors for the people you lead.

The Four Hallmarks of Open-Door Leadership Revisited

Bob Carr, the founder of Executive Adventure, is a good example of an open-door leader. The approach he used in helping me grow professionally illustrates the four skills that a leader needs to open doors of opportunity. These skills were introduced in chapter 1, but it is worth revisiting them to reinforce how essential they are to open-door leadership. Let's briefly walk through each skill, using Bob's approach in opening this door for me as an example.

- **Knowing your employees:** Even when I was hired on as a salesperson, Bob knew that my aspiration was to facilitate team-building programs. He knew that for me to grow and progress, he would have to create a path out of my entry-level sales role and into the role that I desired. Knowing your employees' ambitions and where they hope to end up will ensure that you fit them for the right opportunity.

- **Matching suitedness:** After I proved to Bob, and myself, that I was capable of facilitating more consequential programs, he saw the connection between my skills and capabilities and the outcomes our client (Ford) was trying to achieve. He knew that I was well suited to lead the job. Open-door leaders match a person's skills (or lack thereof) with the opportunities that can make them stronger. As will be explained later, even a person's prior failure can be an indicator that they are well suited for an opportunity.

- **Envisioning desired results:** Bob knew that if he gave me a smaller and less-consequential proving ground (by leading smaller nonprofit programs), my skills would become sharper and I would eventually add more value to our company and the clients we served. He had spent enough quality-development time with me to have a clear vision of the professional I was capable of becoming. Every assignment was a step down the path of helping me live into that vision.

- **Providing ongoing support:** Bob had a stake in supporting and promoting my success every step of the way. He actively coached me. He shared his favorite facilitator questions. He gave me feedback about my performance after soliciting my own. He and I attended client meetings together. His support helped me grow, and my growth benefitted both the company and me. It's not enough to provide a person with an opportunity. You have to support them as they pursue the opportunity too.

For me, Bob was an open-door leader. When I look back on my career, I can connect the dots between my career as a management consultant today and the opportunities that Bob Carr gave me early on. While I may have been "a kid with promise," the promise would have gone unfulfilled if Bob had not given me small and large opportunity proving grounds.

The end result for me is deep gratitude. By opening a door to a proving ground, the open-door leader gains deep loyalty. It makes sense. After experiencing the proving ground, how could you not be grateful to the leader who gave you the access? How could you not be grateful to the leader who gave you your first shot?

Give Me a Break!

Creating other leaders is an essential responsibility of leadership. As a practical reality, the only way to do that is to give others a chance to lead. In other words, you've got to give people a break. People want, and need, opportunities to break away from the past, break free of their routines, break away from the herd, and break into the place that you've already reached.

There's a very strong connection between giving people a break and your legacy as a leader. Consider this list of famous comedians and try to figure out what they all have in common: David Letterman, Jay Leno, Tim Allen, Bill Maher, Rosanne Barr, Joan Rivers, Drew Carey, Ellen DeGeneres, and Jerry Seinfeld. Did you get what—or more accurately who—they have in common?

The answer is Johnny Carson.

During Johnny's reign as the host of *The Tonight Show*, the goal of any up-and-coming comedian was to win Johnny's approval. If he liked your routine, he'd wink and give you the okay sign. If he really liked your act, he'd call you over to sit next to him for some banter. If you "killed" on *The Tonight Show*, your success was virtually assured, which is why comedians were so eager for the chance to prove themselves on Johnny's show. Johnny had an eye for comedic talent. He could spot the diamond in the rough, and he genuinely enjoyed giving budding comics their big break. Johnny opened doors for many comedians we continue to enjoy today. Johnny Carson was an open-door leader.

When you give someone a chance to prove herself, you validate that she is someone worth taking a chance on. Even if she fails, she will learn, grow, and progress in the process. That growth, whether the result of success or failure, will make her more likely to succeed in the future. Thus, as a leader, your job is to keep providing proving-ground opportunities, because that's where the growth happens.

Open-Door Actions and Reflections

Think about the people you're currently leading or influencing at work and then respond to these questions and statements:

1. How could you use your influence to create opportunities for them? Is there someone right now who could use a "break"?

2. Is there someone who has been asking for a chance to take on greater challenges or responsibilities? How could you make that happen?

3. What are some smaller opportunities you could offer as preparation for bigger ones? What proving-ground doors could you open right now?

4. Next, look back over the course of your career. List some people who "gave you a shot."

   • Were there some smaller opportunities that they gave you that led to bigger ones?

   • What doors opened for you because of the interest they took in you?

   • What reflections and insights do you have from these leaders? Are they positive or negative?

5. Drawing on the example you just listed, create a concentric opportunity map like the one below. Write the small opportunities that you received in the smallest circle of the map and then larger ones leading up to the biggest opportunity.

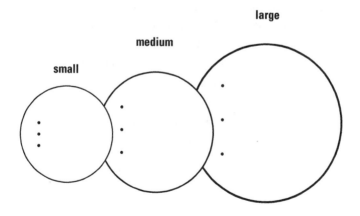

6. Now think about someone you're currently leading. Start with the big opportunity you'd like to create for them. Work your way through the map below. What smaller opportunity could you create in the very near future for that person?

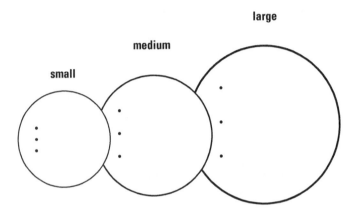

7. Review the four skills required of an open-door leader. What actions could you take to enhance your use of them? What actions can you take, for example, to better get to know the career aspirations of your direct reports?

Chapter 5

The Thought-Shifting Door

Change your thoughts and you change your world.
—Norman Vincent Peale

Not all opportunities are tangible. Some are more mental in nature. In addition to providing people with tangible, skill-developing work opportunities, open-door leaders need to know how to shift people's thinking. Real opportunities can be found in getting people to be more imaginative by freeing them from narrow, negative, or habitual thinking.

This chapter introduces three aspects of bringing about thought shifts. The first involves catching people off guard by disrupting their mental routines. The second involves the use of symbolism, which can help shift people's focus back to the priorities that matter most. The third involves small language changes. There's a big difference between "not bad" and "pretty good"; small word choices can make a big difference in people's thoughts and attitudes.

Use a Barbeque in the Park, Not a Conference Room!

One challenge most leaders face is how to inspire more workplace creativity. There are plenty of clock punchers out there—folks who are physically working but mentally retired. Elevating people to higher standards of performance and inspiring useful ideas requires igniting their imaginations. Open-door leaders are keen to prevent complacency and lethargy. They know that the mental grooves of habit eventually form ruts of routine. When people see things the way they've always seen them, everything stays the same, dulling work to the point of drudgery.

Inspiring creativity and imagination often requires disrupting people's mental routine and catching them off guard. Consider the marketing meetings a large manufacturer of paper plates held to figure out how to reach more customers. To the people who spent most of their working life centered on this commodity product, the answer was simple: discounting! Whenever the company wanted to increase market share, they would simply pump out more Sunday coupons. But the temporary discount-driven boost in market share would often come at the expense of lower profit margins.

As a result, the division's leader wanted his employees to be more imaginative than just defaulting to discounting all the time. He wanted them to remember that they weren't just selling plates, cups, and napkins, they were working for a brand that was deeply connected to the family experience.

To lift his employees out of the rut of discount thinking, the division leader conducted a brainstorming meeting at a beautiful community park near the corporate headquarters. The meeting was different because it was set up as a backyard barbeque. There were picnic tables with red-and-white checkered tablecloths, an outdoor grill sizzling with hotdogs and hamburgers, even outdoor games like horseshoes and tetherball.

Of course there was also something else: lots of the company's plates, cups, and napkins. They weren't just commodities; they were an essential part of the experience. The division's open-door leader used this picnic to help his employees shift their thinking away from commodities and toward values and traditions. They started seeing that on any summer day, their products were smack-dab in the middle of people's backyard barbeques, picnics, and family birthday parties. The products were important because they helped make family time more fun, enjoyable, and worry free. Without the picnic table, grill, and *their products*, a backyard would just be a sorry patch of land behind the house.

Contrast this leader's approach to inspiring people's imagination to the alternative, which you have probably experienced. Your boss likely gathered everyone in the same old meeting room—the one where people usually drone over monthly accounting reports—to get lots of great ideas. You probably had to hunt all over the building to find a flipchart and then search again to find a marker that actually worked. As a bonus, the 2 p.m. meeting was just in time for everyone's after-lunch coma to set in. After everyone arrived, your boss, standing next to a white piece of flipchart paper and holding a black marker, gleefully said, "Okay everyone, let's get creative!"

The quickest way to get stale, retread, and uninspired ideas is to situate everyone where they do their routine work and have routine meetings. When it comes to inspiring great ideas, the climate you create to gather those ideas matters a lot. Any boss can hold a boring meeting in a tired conference room. By contrast, any boss can also hold an inspiring gathering at the local park, but few do. If you want uncommon ideas, don't choose common approaches.

By choosing to get people outside their thinking routines and away from the four-walled environment of their workplace, the division leader in the first example helped shift people's thinking for the better. When they started percolating new marketing and product ideas, the word "discounting" never came up. Instead, they started talking about creative marketing campaigns designed to inspire the feelings of a warm summer afternoon. They talked about partnering with an outdoor grill company. They talked about designing new "summer flower" borders for their plates and napkins. They talked about creating an interactive website where customers could swap their favorite picnic recipes. By shifting people's thinking and getting them away from the ordinary work environment, the open-door leader opened up a space for them to think in a more inspired way.

Host a Dinner Party at Pearl Harbor?

One of the most effective ways open-door leaders get people to think differently is by using symbolism. For instance, the CEO of a large fashion design company who decided to inspire more courageous behavior among his retail stores' general managers. Thanks to blowing past their yearly sales goals, the general managers had earned a five-day trip to Hawaii for the annual GM conference. Concerned that the company's very success could plant the seeds of complacency, the CEO decided to host a dinner in a very unexpected location—on the deck of USS *Missouri* in Pearl Harbor.

The "Mighty Mo" is one of the most famous battleships of all time. It joined the Pacific fleet during World War II after being christened by Harry Truman's daughter; fought at Iwo Jima and Okinawa; and suffered, but withstood, a kamikaze attack. Later, it fought in both the Korean and Gulf wars. Perhaps most famously, the deck of the Mighty Mo was where, in front of Gen. Douglas MacArthur and Adm. Chester Nimitz, the Japanese signed the Instrument of Surrender.

That evening, under Mo's gigantic guns, the CEO thanked everyone for their hard work and reminded them about the importance of courage, persistence, and preventing complacency. Although they were very, very successful thus far, the headwinds of competition were strong and unrelenting. Just as the Mighty Mo never surrendered in the face of hardship, neither should they. He showed them that they weren't just working for a fashion company, they were fighting in a fiercely competitive marketplace, and nothing short of their best would keep sales in tip-top shape and preserve the company's rich tradition of success. The out-of-the-ordinary location was perfectly aligned, symbolically, with the message the CEO wanted to send about the dangers of getting caught off guard by complacency and that now was not the time to let up.

Symbols: You Weave the Meaning

Using symbols is a powerful way to help shift people's thinking. Open-door leaders have to speak about more than just the mechanics of the business, they have to show people how their jobs fit into a larger context. They need be weavers of meaning and significance to help their employees draw the connections between their seemingly small jobs and the more extraordinary purpose they're helping to advance. By providing symbolic reference points, open-door leaders can inspire their employees to view their world differently. Here are some other examples of this approach.

The division head of a large international hotel chain hosts a series of small meetings in a hotel suite at their flagship location, which are focused on "owning the sleep market." A medical doctor who specializes in healthy sleep habits attends to help prompt new ideas.

Every year on March 4 the leader of a creative consulting firm closes shop so his employees can dedicate themselves to an idea that they find personally inspiring. They are encouraged to "march forth" toward their idea.

The leader of a company that's aiming to transform its culture hosts a meeting at the Fernbank Museum of Natural History in Atlanta. A world-renowned cultural anthropologist speaks to the attendees about what strengthens and weakens cultures.

Every other month, the director of career development at a large Chicago-based company hosts a small meeting to deepen the impact of the company's leadership-development program. The gathering is held at the Catalyst Ranch, a creative venue designed for ideation and brainstorming meetings. Catalyst Ranch is like a Warholian psychedelic curio shop, but with flip-charts! The groovy atmosphere promotes imaginative "what-if" thinking.

For a Better Result, Shift the Language

Shifting people's thinking doesn't require grandiose gestures on the part of the open-door leader. Sometimes just making small language shifts affect how people define themselves. Take, for example, the owner of a $4 billion construction company, who wanted his division heads to do less managing and more leading. For decades, the division heads had been called business group managers. Was it really any wonder then that their focus was on managing their divisions? However, they really needed to focus less on internal operational issues (management) and more on external opportunities, such as developing business with clients (leadership). So the owner did something simple but important. He changed the job title and, by definition, the expectation and focus of their job. Now the division heads are called business group *leaders*.

Opening Heads

Part of your job as an open-door leader is to keep people from thinking in ways that are counterproductive to themselves and the organization. You need to open the thought-shifting door. Catch people off guard, disrupt their mental routines, use symbols, and make small changes in language. These are great tools for shifting thinking. There are countless other ways, too. It doesn't matter what you do, as long as you get people to think positively, constructively, and productively.

Open-Door Actions and Reflections

1. What symbol or metaphor best resembles what your organization is trying to achieve?

   - How could you use this symbolic reference to communicate in a powerful or compelling way? Be specific in explaining how you'll use the symbol/metaphor.

2. What are some ways that your organization typically tries to inspire creative ideas?

   - What about this approach works well?

   - What opportunities for improvement exist?

3. Use the framework on the next page to assess your goals.

   - Identify a few one-word examples of unproductive or outdated thinking (apathetic, fearful) in the first column.

   - List the healthier and more productive words you'd like reflected in people's attitudes (initiative, courageous) in the second column.

   - In the third column, list the actions you could take to shift people from the first column to the second column (jointly set ambitious goals, institute temporary job rotations).

   - Finally, and most importantly, set a deadline for finishing each action!

Unproductive Thinking	Productive Thinking	Thought-Shifting Actions	Action Deadline

Chapter 6

The Door to a Second Chance

Having a second chance makes
you want to work even harder.
—Tia Mowry

The company's owner will neither confirm nor deny that he is Mr. Fusion. Many people think he is. Then again, maybe he isn't. But he sure could be. Maybe.

If he is Mr. Fusion, he's one of the most famous computer hackers in the world—part James Bond, part Mark Zuckerberg. He's part of an elite group of coders who are capable of hacking into the most sensitive government systems. He did so singlehandedly.

Even if he isn't Mr. Fusion, he is deeply, deeply involved in cyber warfare. *BusinessWeek* called the company he founded the "premier cyber-arms dealer." Its expertise is in *zero-day exploits*, which is geek-speak for taking advantage of computer software or application vulnerabilities that are unknown even to the software's developers. The company is comprised of "white hat" hackers who develop code to exploit security holes to conduct international clandestine surveillance operations. Sometimes they go further, conducting all out cyber attacks against bad-guy nations. Be glad they're on our side.

Mr. Fusion's company is into some wild, jaw-dropping stuff. And some very important people sit on the company's board of directors—people whose names you would instantly recognize for their spy credentials or high military rank.

But Mr. Fusion, if he is Mr. Fusion, is only able to do what he does because an open-door leader gave him a second chance.

How Would You Handle a Hacker?

In 1989, during the first Gulf War, the Pentagon became increasingly concerned that foreign enemies or terrorist groups would exploit U.S. defense systems. The concern was especially pronounced because they had caught a Washington, D.C., teenager hacking into the air force's computer systems just days before Iraq invaded Kuwait. In the dark world of the hacker community, the kid was known only by his chat-room handle: Mr. Fusion.

Consider what you would do if you caught a teenage punk hacking into some of the most sensitive computer systems in the world—systems that, in the wrong hands, could destabilize the nation's security system, or worse. Would you throw the book at the hacker, sending him to a maximum security prison for the rest of his life? Would you exact a stronger punishment? Maybe expel him from the United States and set him up in a dank prison in the Czech Republic? Or, would you look for the opportunities this "problem child" presented?

Think for a second about the unique skills that Mr. Fusion had acquired. Wouldn't you rather have these skills working for you instead of against you? What if you could replicate his skills? Or, what if Mr. Fusion could introduce you to other Mr. Fusions out there?

The key to being an open-door leader is finding the opportunity in situations that others view as problems. That Mr. Fusion broke into a military computer system was a problem, to be sure, on an international scale. But it was also a gigantic opportunity. Skills like his were exceedingly rare, but the uses for those skills, from a national security standpoint, were growing. Hackers are more imaginative, clever, and devious than graduates of computer science programs. Their talents are too exceptional to find through the traditional means of recruiting—hackers aren't recruited; they're caught, and then, only rarely. When you catch one, you have a decision to make: opportunity or punishment?

An Open-Door Leader Strikes a Deal

The open-door leader in this story is Special Agent Jim Christy, the chief of computer crime investigations with the air force's Office of Security Investigations at the time of the breach. He struck a win/win deal with Mr. Fusion and shifted the situation from a problem to an opportunity. Special Agent Christy agreed testify on Mr. Fusion's behalf at the criminal sentencing. In exchange, Mr. Fusion agreed to help the air force secure its computer systems by hacking into as many computers as he could. He would get to keep doing what he loved to do, just in a way that was constructive. In the spirit of the patriotic code crackers of World War II, Mr. Fusion was no longer a hacker, he was a *cracker*.

Christy set him up with a workspace and all the resources he needed to go to work. As agents watched his every keystroke, Mr. Fusion was able to breach more than 200 air force systems within three weeks. Eventually, using Mr. Fusion's methods and tools, along with skills from other members of the hacker community, a government team of crackers was able to access 88 percent of all military systems. More importantly, once the vulnerabilities were exposed, the systems could be made more secure. All this happened because Special Agent Christy gave Mr. Fusion a second chance.

Strategic Forgiveness

The essence of a second chance is strategic forgiveness. This is not the forgiveness in the spiritual sense; it is the forgiveness of an opportunistic nature. It is the kind of forgiveness that, after weighing all the factors and grievances, recognizes that the person who gets a second chance often becomes deeply loyal and committed to walking on a nobler path. By giving someone a second chance, an open-door leader creates the opportunity for a conversion experience, allowing for healthier and more productive choices. There is a risk of getting burned by giving a second chance, but the opportunities outweigh the risk if you successfully convert someone from destructive behavior to constructive behavior.

Mr. Fusion's story extends beyond helping the air force. If we are to believe the rumors, he is now a productive, tax-paying member of society whose clandestine company employs more than 50 white hat computer-hacking patriots who work for the good of national security.

When a Second Chance Is Worth the Risk

An open-door leader has to be very thoughtful about when to give someone a second chance. For example, giving an embezzler a second chance would be stupid. Letting someone off the hook for sexual harassment would not only be immoral, it would probably get both of you fired.

So, how do you decide who deserves a second chance? Mercy should be reserved for people who:

- made an honest and legal mistake
- approached the situation thoughtfully and logically, but the outcome just didn't work out (good reasons, bad outcome)

- made a mistake out of ignorance, not malice (such as a young employee who barges into the CEO's office to ask for a raise)

- suffer after a career setback, but have a long track record of adding value to the company

- are deeply embarrassed for their mistakes and likely to retain the lesson for the duration of their careers.

Are You a "No-Chance" Leader?

Many leaders are quick to punish and slow to forgive. When a worker makes a mistake and begs for mercy, this kind of leader says, "No way!" and then rubs the worker's nose in the mistake, as if she was an errant dog in need of punishment. No-chance leaders seem to take pleasure in the role of punisher, reveling in leveling harsh judgments. Their power derives from their ability to cause pain.

Open-door leaders, conversely, are powerful because they opt first for mercy and use punishment only as a last resort. By choosing forgiveness over iron-fisted punishment, the open-door leader creates a learning opportunity. Thus the person who has been traveling down the wrong road stands the best chance of getting on the right path.

How would you react if an employee lost a client, got the data wrong, came in over budget, or dropped the ball in some other way? Would you explode? Would you mentally write him off for good and hold the mistake against him forever more? Would you stew with resentment?

What kind of example are you setting for others by the way you handle (or mishandle) mistakes? While no leader should tolerate habitual mistakes, all leaders should expect some mess-ups . . . even from themselves. Mistakes, small and big, often provide the best learning opportunities, however, the opportunity vanishes if the punishment far outweighs the crime.

Open-Door Actions and Reflections

1. Think of a mistake you've made.

   - What was it?

   - How did people label you after you made it?

   - Who gave you a second chance along the way?

   - How did the second chance impact who you are today?

2. How do you handle or mishandle mistakes?

   - What was the most recent mistake that one of your direct reports made?

   - Were you able to turn the mistake into a learning opportunity?

   - How did you do it?

3. Have you been harboring a resentment or grudge against someone at work?

    - What would it take for you to forgive them?
    - What are the benefits—to them and you—that might make forgiveness a strategic choice?

Chapter 7

Opening Doors for Others

*I believe that we are here for each other,
not against each other. Everything comes from
an understanding that you are a gift in my life—
whoever you are, whatever our differences.*
—John Denver

Opening doors for *Others* is an essential job for any leader. Unfortunately, too often, leaders don't treat everyone equally. They have a tendency to promote people who are just like them in gender, ethnicity, sexual orientation, and disposition. It's just plain easier to develop a common bond and kinship with people who look, talk, act, and think like you do. It's also just plain dangerous.

While gravitating toward members of one's own tribe is understandable, if leaders surround themselves with duplicates, cliques form, groupthink takes over, and the people least like the leader—called *Others* in this chapter— get resentful and restless. When leaders exclude Others, they also exclude the varied perspectives and ideas that could help the leaders make better and more imaginative decisions.

Who are these Others the leaders are excluding? Anyone who doesn't fit the predominant profile of the folks at the top—people from outside the dominant tribe.

The vast majority of senior leaders across nearly all organizations in the United States and Europe are white men. That's not an indictment; it's a fact. The challenge is that it's not natural for white, male leaders to open doors for women, blacks, other non-whites, people with disabilities, or homosexuals. Excluding these Others from the top ranks likely has less to do with duplicity or racism (at least consciously), than it does with obliviousness and ignorance. Yet the impact is the same. Qualified people don't get a fair chance to succeed, which harms both them and the organization.

Them's Not Like Us

Many leadership-development programs focus on next-level leaders and are designed to develop the bench strength of the folks who will someday be running the organization—high-potential successors. The best of these programs involve a rigorous intake process: bosses nominate program candidates, who then complete surveys and assessments before they audition for inclusion in the program. But regardless of how objective and rigorous the intake process is, the selected candidates often resemble the very people who nominated them in the first place—their leaders. When this happens—and it happens a lot—the most senior leaders would be wise to cast a wider net to include less obvious high-potential candidates. Otherwise they are in danger of replicating themselves and losing the advantages that a differing perspective can yield.

To be clear, most leaders are not consciously racist or bigoted. In fact, my experience working with many leaders has been largely the opposite. Most are decent, ethical people who simply default to creating duplicates at the top. They just need a lot of reminders—from shareholders, advocacy groups, outside consultants, and so on—to include Others. Including less-obvious candidates during the screening process lowers the risk of missing a talented gem who could have shined as a leader.

Open-Door Leaders Create Opportunities for Women

Without active and intentional support from leaders, especially white male leaders, the opportunity landscape for Others is much smaller and restricted. For example, according to a 2009 White House Project Report on benchmarking women's leadership, women make up roughly 52 percent of the labor market worldwide. However, they only account for about 18 percent of top leadership positions across industry sectors in the United States. This is despite the fact that almost 90 percent of the general public consistently reports being comfortable having women in top leadership roles. What makes this disparity particularly troublesome is that according to a recent, although controversial, study of 7,280 leaders conducted by Zenger Folkman and featured in the *Harvard Business Review* article, "Are Women Better Leaders Than Men?," women often outperform their male counterparts in top-level jobs. The study suggests that any organization that cares about profits and performance would be well served to include more women at the top.

To be sure, women have made great strides in cracking the proverbial glass ceiling. Twenty-three women (4.6 percent) hold CEO positions at Fortune 500 companies, including Virginia Rometty at IBM, Mary Barra at GM, and Marissa Mayer at Yahoo. But while the glass ceiling isn't as thick as it used to be, it still exists. History suggests that women will not be able to fully dismantle the ceiling by sheer force of will and talent without the active contribution and cooperation of male leaders. The reality is that men largely hold the keys to the boardroom and C-suite. So if they aren't actively creating opportunities for women—a very large group of Others—male leaders run the risk of becoming opportunity obstructionists.

One difference between men and women at work is that a man can climb the corporate ladder based on hard work, ambition, and merit, with very few obstructions. There's almost nothing stopping him if he's effective enough. Women can demonstrate all these attributes and still find diminishing opportunities as they progress, through no fault of their own. At some point, it is likely, a woman might not get any farther without a man opening a door for her. This isn't paternalism. I am not suggesting that women are weak damsels who need men to rescue them. I *am* suggesting that by being overly attentive to their own tribe, male leaders routinely, and often unconsciously, obstruct opportunities for women by treating them as Others.

Being an open-door leader means giving special attention to opening doors for people who are not like you. Fortunately there are some positive role models to follow. According to the *USA Today* article, "Often, Men Help Women Get to the Corner Office," Andrea Jung, the former CEO and current board chair of Avon, credits James Preston, her predecessor, with opening the C-suite door to her. During her first interview with James, she noticed that there was an interesting plaque behind his desk. It bore four footprints: an ape, a barefoot man, a wingtip shoe, and a high-heeled shoe. Its title was "The Evolution of Leadership."

Andrea is not alone in being an Other who benefitted from the progressiveness of an open-door leader. According to a survey mentioned in the same *USA Today* article, 33 out of 34 female CEOs mentioned a man when asked to identify the mentor who had the most influence on their career. Interestingly, most of these men have daughters. Greg Palmer—mentor of Jill Ater, founder of a company called 10 till 2—explained to *USA Today* that, "Having daughters, seeing firsthand their struggles, fears and dreams, it makes it easier to relate to other women and their struggles, fears and dreams." Greg has three daughters, which seems to be a factor in his efforts to make the Other less "other."

From One Man to an Other

Otherness diminishes rapidly when you can relate to the Other's plight. Consider Marshall Carter, the past chair of the New York Stock Exchange and mentor to Deborah Ellinger, president of Restoration Hardware. In addition to having two daughters, Marshall is a Vietnam vet, a former marine, and a recipient of the Navy Cross. When he returned home and sought employment after two tours as an officer in Vietnam, 85 companies rejected him, despite his master's degree in operations research and systems analysis. His stellar resume made no difference; the public's distaste for the war had turned him into an Other.

As mentioned in chapter 2, an open-door leader sees opportunities where everyone else sees problems. Having experienced firsthand the humiliation of being obstructed from opportunities for which he was qualified, Marshall was determined to not block opportunities for others who worked for him. Even in the early 1980s, when he was a senior executive at Chase Manhattan Bank, nine of the 12 vice presidents who reported to him were women. Summing up Marshall's open-door leadership approach, Deborah told *USA Today*, "He understands what it means to be an outsider."

Even Others Have Others

Each of us has an Other somewhere in our lives. Others are members of minority groups—not minority solely as in "black or Latino," but as in the minority within your own organization. Others are those who represent a much smaller percentage within an organization. Just as the needs and concerns of a woman working in a male-dominated workplace are unique, so too are those of a male worker working in a female-dominated workplace. The same holds true for an older employee working in a tech start-up company, surrounded by thumb-tapping, text-sending millennials. In each case, the leader needs to pay special attention to make sure that doors are opening for everyone, not only those who are just like the leader.

The challenge in leading Others is that you often don't know what you don't know. Unless you directly seek out perspective, input, and feedback from Others, you won't know what their unique needs and concerns are and it will be hard to create opportunities for them. Fortunately, this is surprisingly easy to do. Just move toward them. Read blogs and newsletters that are written for these groups. Find out what causes they champion. Listen to podcasts from luminaries they respect. Most importantly, and to prevent stereotyping, spend time getting to know the individuals you're leading, even if their lives are very different from your own. Don't be interrogative. Just follow your curiosity and ask questions in the way a five-year-old would—innocently and with purity of heart.

A good example of spending time getting to know rank-and-file workers comes from BJ Gallagher Hateley, author of *Peacock in the Land of Penguins*, one of the best books ever written about working with Others. During her years as the manager of training and development at the *Los Angeles Times*, BJ worked for a senior executive named Tom Johnson. One evening, while she was giving a workshop for the pressmen who worked at night printing the newspaper, Tom popped into the room and said, "What's going on in here tonight? How's everybody doing?" The pressmen were happy to see him, and BJ was totally surprised. Keep in mind that Tom wasn't just a senior executive, he was *the* senior executive—the newspaper's publisher. Yet here he was at 10 at night making small talk with the rank-and-file pressmen.

After Tom left, BJ asked the guys, "Does he do that often?" And they said, "Yes, he does. He often comes by late at night, after he's been to some corporate evening event, the theater, or some business dinner. He comes in, picks up a copy of the paper as it's coming off the press, and talks with the guys for a while before he goes home."

One has to imagine that Tom, who would go on to become president of CNN for more than a decade, benefitted from those meetings with Others as much as they did. It was he, after all, who was the true Other in that situation. In any company, the CEO is always a minority of one. Too many leaders at the top cloister themselves in the executive suites, where the rarefied air can distance them from the people who do the actual work. Few things are as dangerous for a leader as becoming out of touch with the people's needs and wants. Open-door leaders like Tom Johnson, however, strive to tear down whatever walls exist between them and their workforce. When they do, *otherness* becomes less important than *togetherness*.

Open-Door Actions and Reflections

1. Identify a time in your career when you felt like an Other.

   - Describe the situation and the emotions that come up for you when you remember it. Ultimately, how was this situation resolved?

   - Did someone play the role of open-door leader in this situation? If so, what opportunity did they create for you?

   - How could you pay that door-opening forward?

2. Identify two colleagues who are Others to you. Pick one from each gender. Take them to lunch, separately, simply to get to know them better. Afterward, see if there are some doors that would be worth opening for them.

3. Find out if your organization has a diversity office or function. If so:

   - Spend an hour there getting educated about what the organization is doing to create a level playing field for Others.

   - Review the data and statistics about the composition of your workforce, including the top team and the board of directors.

   - Meet with the diversity manager to ask how you can contribute to the organization's diversity goals.

Chapter 8

The Door to Personal Transformation

When we quit thinking primarily about ourselves and our own self-preservation, we undergo a truly heroic transformation of consciousness.
—Joseph Campbell

==

Some executives think that leadership is only about momentum and results. But even a slave master can crack the whip hard enough to get people working harder and faster. The best leaders do more than move us forward. They also help us rise above who we are so that we can move closer to the person we can become. Open-door leaders lift us up. They elevate our standards, ethics, and performance by creating opportunities for us to transform ourselves.

Human growth and development requires constantly advancing from who you are to who you want to become. In order to do that, you first must discover who you truly are, and this is a big challenge for most people. Without knowing who you are, how can you ever know what to transform about yourself? Open-door leaders promote personal transformation by helping us know ourselves better, by holding us accountable to our own potential, and sometimes, by hitting us upside the head with the left hook of reality. The most powerful means of promoting personal transformation, though, is through the examples they set for us as role models.

Role Modeling Personal Transformation

There is no more powerful influencer on the culture of a workplace than the behavior of its leaders. Leaders set the behavioral tone of the organization, so it's important that they keep evolving and growing. This means purposefully doing things that are uncomfortable that create opportunities for their own development. It's much easier to follow people who embody the values they are asking us to live up to.

Consider Cal, who inherited a multimillion dollar business upon the sudden death of his father. Being only in his late 20s, and under intense pressure not to let the business fail, Cal overcompensated for his lack of leadership experience through heavy-handed and authoritarian leader behavior. Hundreds of people's livelihoods, he thought, were depending on his not failing. He was full of fear and he transmitted that fear to others in the form of harsh leadership.

It's hard to get through to a hardhead, but it can be done. In Cal's case, it came in the form of a 360-degree leadership-feedback survey. Exhausted from his work pressures and perplexed by the frustrations of leading the company, Cal signed up to attend a 7 Habits class at the Sundance Resort. The class would be led by Stephen Covey, author of *The 7 Habits of Highly Effective People*, one of the most influential leadership books of all time.

As part of the Covey program, Cal received a 360-degree feedback assessment, whereby his direct reports gave candid and anonymous feedback about his leadership style. The feedback Cal got was startling, especially the raw, qualitative comments at the end. Words like "dominating," "obnoxious," and "offensive" jumped off the page. Curiously, one word came up over and over: afraid. That word, in particular, stung because Cal knew that it was true. He was afraid of failing and letting everyone down. He had tried to cloak his fear with his commanding presence. Clearly, it hadn't worked and the 360 provided the proof.

Sometimes the best thing that can happen to a leader is for them to experience humiliation, because humiliation is the birthplace of humility. The embarrassment and shame that Cal felt after seeing the results of the survey tenderized his hardness. He was now ready to accept that he needed help, that he couldn't just will success into being. He was failing alright. Not because he wasn't working hard enough, but because he wasn't bringing people with him.

Cal set out to be a better leader. After attending the Covey program, he became a certified Covey instructor and brought the concepts back to his company. Some of the company's senior executives also got certified and, along with Cal, led workshops for the entire workforce. Based on the success of the workshops, Cal dramatically increased the training budget, which allowed for other training opportunities. Finally, after conducting a series of focus groups to get the input of the workforce, the company created its first-ever mission statement.

Cal had changed for the better, and people could see it. He dictated less and asked for input more. He spent time talking about the company's strategy and the opportunities the strategy was focused on creating. He walked the halls and dropped in on people, just to see how things were going. He also said "thank you" . . . a lot.

As Cal changed, so did the climate of the workplace. Work was still work, and the work still had to get done. But now it was getting done with enthusiasm and positive energy, not foot dragging and bellyaching. Cal's optimism gave way to a general workplace optimism. The company simply became a more positive place to be.

Inspiring Your Own Personal Transformation

It's hard to be an open-door leader if your mental door is closed. Transformation, personally and organizationally, needs to start with you. Here are some ways to bring about your own transformation.

- Get a mentor inside the organization and hire a coach outside the organization.

- Go through a 360-degree feedback process.

- Devise and recite a daily mantra, like "calm confidence," "be courageous," or "discomfort equals growth."

- Write a gratitude list at the start of each day.

- Sign up to do regular service work, such as joining Big Brothers Big Sisters or building a house with Habitat for Humanity.

- Start each day with five minutes of silent meditation.

- Take a yearly retreat at a transformational learning center, like the Esalen Institute at Big Sur, California.

- Change your insides by first changing your outside— this could include geting an image makeover, changing your clothes, or trying out new hairstyle.

- Experience the world by taking a solo trip abroad.

- Get a personal trainer and/or sign up for a rigorous fitness program.

- Take a three-month sabbatical and get reacquainted with who you always wanted to be.

Holding the Door Open

Sometimes opening the door for transformation is simply a matter of pointing a person in the direction of their potential and holding steady until they reach it. Steve, a project manager in a large commercial building company, is a great example. Steve had a enjoyed a successful career and was poised for a bright future—until he suffered a crisis of confidence when a project he had led tanked and lost millions of dollars. There were a host of reasons why the project went south, including misestimating the cost of the work, underbidding the project, performing in an entirely new market, and a fickle and unreasonable client. If anything, Steve's leadership had prevented the project from being an even bigger loss. But he didn't view it that way. He personalized the failure. As a result, he started to doubt himself and became much more hesitant and much less confident.

Fortunately, Steve worked for a seasoned open-door leader. His boss, Wayne, had experienced a similar crisis earlier in his career, so he knew what Steve was going through. He could tell that Steve wanted to scale back his career a bit, become less visible, and maybe take on smaller projects for a while. Wayne knew, from his own experience, that what Steve really needed was to take on another large and complex project. Why? For two reasons. First, if Steve allowed himself to shrink, he might get comfortable with a lower standard of achievement. Second, Wayne knew that

Steve was capable of so much more than he had shown thus far. Wayne believed in Steve's potential even more than he did. If there's one thing gray-haired leaders develop a keen eye for, it's talent. Despite the recent setback, Wayne knew that Steve was a really talented guy.

So what did Wayne do? He put Steve in charge of a large, complex project the company had just landed. It was one of the largest in the company's history, and a lot of money was at stake. If that weren't enough, the project was a joint venture with a partner that had no prior history with Steve's company. Oh yeah, and the project was on the opposite side of the country.

Notice that what made Steve the right choice for the new opportunity wasn't that he had been successful before. It was the opposite. He was suited for the opportunity *because* of his recent failure and his need to overcome it.

Steve pleaded with Wayne to pick someone else. Wayne listened patiently and then said, "No." Steve protested that he might lose the company money. Wayne said, "You'd better not." Steve said the move would be tough on his family. Wayne said, "Bring 'em." Steve said, "I'm afraid." Wayne said, "You should be."

Once you open a door of opportunity for somebody, you may need to stop them from closing it. Wayne knew that what Steve truly needed was redemption; in the eyes of his company, yes, but more importantly, in his view of himself. Steve would never hold himself accountable to who he was capable of becoming as a professional if Wayne let him settle for becoming a smaller self. Leaders fail. It comes with the territory. If anything, Wayne believed, Steve had earned a stripe that he hadn't yet claimed. Leading a big, hairy, complex job would be just what Steve needed to capitalize on the lessons he had learned from his prior failure. So Wayne refused to let Steve close the door. He kept Steve accountable to his own potential.

It's important to understand that Wayne didn't just dump the opportunity in Steve's lap and then cut and run—he was deeply involved every step of the way. Steve didn't take over the leadership helm instantaneously, some baton passing had to happen first. Wayne and Steve worked closely to shape the relationship with the new venture partner. They sifted through the project contract and estimates; attended client meetings; and traveled to, and presented at, the quarterly division meetings back at the company headquarters. They were in it together. Steve's opportunity to reclaim his confidence was Wayne's opportunity to leave a positive and lasting imprint on future leader.

Ways to Increase Accountability

Accountability is an all-or-nothing proposition. Either you are or you aren't. Your job as an open-door leader is to create an environment where everyone, including you, is held accountable.

Here are some tips for increasing accountability.

- Write down explicit expectations about the activities, deliverables, and deadlines that have to be achieved; no vagaries allowed.

- List all the excuses you can think of for why the work won't get done; then list actions to remedy those excuses upfront.

- Clarify the rewards for success and the consequences for failure.

- Post the expectations in a place where they can continuously be seen and referred to.

- Make sure everyone is aware of each other's specific assignments—create social pressure to succeed.

- Establish a schedule for frequent progress reviews, and increase the frequency if progress slips.

- After all the activities, deliverables, and deadlines have been met (or not), conduct a lessons-learned meeting to capture improvement ideas for future assignments.

By not letting up and by always being on point, Steve slowly reclaimed his confidence. As of right now, he is successfully leading the large joint venture. And, with Steve's help, Wayne is working on landing an even bigger project in the same area.

Could You Be a Velvet Hammer?

One of the most effective ways to increase the likelihood of a personal transformation in others is to give straightforward feedback. Open-door leader give us the kind of feedback that takes courage to deliver and even more courage to hear, and personal transformation is almost impossible without it. Consider, for example, this story of a middle manager whose boss, one of the most respected people in the company, gave him some hard-hitting feedback that most people wouldn't have the courage to give. One of the reasons everyone admired and respected the boss was his way of being a *velvet hammer*—he could deliver feedback in a way that would make you pay attention without putting up your defenses. During the middle manager's performance review, after talking about all the things that he was doing well, his boss said, "There is one more thing that I have to tell you before you go. There's something that I'm just starting to notice, and I'm concerned that others will start to notice too. It can become a real drag on your career unless you deal with it now. You're becoming a brown noser."

Ouch! Humiliated, the manager did what any brown noser would do: he tried to laugh it off. "What do you mean, boss? By the way, I meant to tell you that I really like your new tie!" But his boss didn't laugh. He wouldn't let this conversation drift into the shallow waters. What he said next made all the difference: "Listen, you don't have to laugh at my jokes harder than they are funny. That's not only dishonest; it's manipulative. If you just agree with everything I say you'll be of no real value to me. You're a smart guy with a strong imagination. Rely on your own creativity and ideas to get ahead, not on kissing up to people like me."

Ten years after receiving that hard-to-hear feedback, the middle manager considers it the single most important conversation he had in his entire career. His boss essentially gave him permission to care less about what others thought about him. He had been a people pleaser since he was a kid, not because he genuinely cared about others, but because he liked being liked. By schmoosing you, he could get you to like him, and if he could get you to like him, he might be able to get you to do what he wanted—for his benefit, not yours. His boss's tough feedback helped shift him from unconfident inauthenticity to confident authenticity. It helped him become more of a truth teller, which is supremely important to career advancement. He learned to assert his opinions and ideas in a more muscular way, which transformed the development and advancement of his career.

Some people pride themselves on being brutally honest. But brutality almost always puts up people's defenses. The open-door leader provides feedback in a way that gets through to people so they can put the feedback to work and transform their behavior. The balance is one of assertiveness and diplomacy. Before delivering tough feedback, be thoughtful about what you want to say. Make sure it is absorbable and digestible so that your words will be met with reception and not defensiveness. Being a velvet hammer is not about making them feel ashamed of themselves or afraid of you. The point is to communicate assertively and respectably so that the other person benefits from the feedback. Deliver your honesty without brutality.

How a Follower Made Me a Leader

Being a boss does not make one a leader, at least in the sense of an open-door leader. When it comes to creating opportunities for personal transformation, the term "leader" has less to do with hierarchy and more to do with the influence you bring to bear on people and situations. With a little courage, anyone at any level can be a leader. In the preface I mentioned that my journey toward becoming a leadership-development practitioner began when a courageous employee told me what a lousy leader I was. He told me this after I had pushed him to the point that he was ready to quit.

At the time I was the show director of an aquatic stage and stunt show put on by the U.S. High Diving Team. The employee and I were also high divers in the show. Each day we would climb a 100-foot-high dive ladder and hurl ourselves toward the pool below, rushing down at speeds in excess of 50 miles per hour into a pool that was 10 feet deep. In addition to performing our death-defying dives, often before crowds of 2,000 people, we also performed Olympic-style dives, a comedy routine, and dangerous double-dive stunts. I'm not being overly dramatic when I tell you that we could have easily been killed on the job.

One day, after what I considered a subpar performance, I ripped into the team like General Patton. I told them that only chumps could put on a show like that. I told them that if they couldn't get with the program, I'd ditch them for divers who could. I told them that they made me ashamed to be their boss. Then I told them to get out of my face because looking at them disgusted me.

After my little tirade, one of the divers stayed behind. He looked me straight in the eye and said, "Listen, Treasurer, who do you think you are? Where do you get off talking to us like that? Do you think that by berating us and making us feel small you will earn our respect? All you do is harp on everyone's mistakes. What's your goal, dude, to make us afraid of you? At what cost? People hate working for you. If you talk to us like that again, I'll walk. I respect myself too much to let you treat me that badly."

The truth only hurts if it should. Hearing the employee's words was painful, because deep down I knew that he was right. I wasn't being a leader; I was being a jerk. The truth was that I had no confidence as a leader at all. I had no idea how to lead, so I adopted the style of my previous boss, and the boss before that. I took up the most heavy-handed aspects of leaders that I had experienced going all the way back to my first leader role model: my father. I was basically channeling my dad, or at least my dad when he was angry. I had no idea who I was, authentically, as a leader. My employee's words confronted me with that reality. But it was exactly what I needed to prompt me to take an interest in the concept of leadership.

Very few people have the courage to give their boss upward feedback. Respecting authority is one of our earliest lessons. So, when faced with an abhorrent boss, most people bite their tongue, which only further enables the abhorrent behavior. In this case, however, the employee had reached his tipping point. The risk of telling me the hard truth on the ever-so-slim chance that I might actually change was less dangerous than letting me stay a world-class jackass. His courage in giving me the raw feedback that I needed to hear (but cringed at hearing) helped trigger a personal transformation.

I began to reflect on the leader I had been versus the one I wanted to be. I started reading books on leadership and team building and, as a result, saw my team's performance improve. I came across the term "organization development" and decided to pursue a graduate degree in that subject. I wrote my thesis on leadership, which gave me my first taste of writing a book-sized manuscript. I can draw a very straight line from the uncomfortable but courageous feedback that diver gave me years ago to the book that you're reading at this moment. In a very direct way, his feedback resulted in the life I live today as a leadership writer, speaker, and consultant. Without his courage, there's a very good chance that I would have gone on to other leadership roles in other organizations, doing a lot of damage to a lot of people in the process. That feedback became my opportunity to change for the better. Even though I was his boss, he served as my open-door leader, because his raw feedback instigated my personal transformation.

Open-Door Leaders Move Us Toward Our Better Selves

Socrates advised us to "know thyself." It is, of course, very good advice, because it is hard to change yourself if you have no idea who you really are. But knowing yourself and transforming yourself based solely on introspection is next to impossible. Open-door leaders serve us best when they help us see ourselves in a different way. By being a good role model, opening the doors to allow us to experience transformation, holding us accountable to our own potential, and giving us direct and diplomatic feedback, open-door leaders help us transform from the person we are to the person we're capable of becoming.

Open-Door Actions and Reflections

1. Identify at least one leader who helped bring about a personal shift for you.

   • What was the shift?

- Why did you need it?
- What did the leader do to help bring it about?

2. List the names of a few people who might consider you an open-door leader.

   - What shifts would they say you helped bring about for them?

3. Think back to a time in your career when someone gave you tough feedback.

   - What did they say to you?
   - How did you react?
   - In what ways did this feedback impact you?

4. Identify one person who needs some feedback that you've been avoiding giving.

   - Why are you avoiding it?
   - What shift might your feedback help that person make?
   - How could you deliver the feedback in a way that preserves the dignity of the person, yet still gets the point across?
   - How could you be a "velvet hammer"?

Chapter 9

The Door to Your Open Heart

The minute a person whose word means a great deal to others dares to take the open-hearted and courageous way, many others follow.
—**Marian Anderson**

Do you care about me? This is what people want to know when they work for you. They may not say it directly, but it is the core question that defines the relationship between you and the people you lead. When people believe the answer is "yes," they will be more committed to their work, and to you. But when they think the answer is "no," their commitment to their job and their loyalty to you will suffer.

To be a leader means getting results. But when the drive for results monopolizes a leader's attention, people become the lesser priority. When a leader cares more about the "ends" (results) and less about the "means" (people), he becomes susceptible to treating people like objects. You'll hear it in the his language—he'll refer to people as "resources," as if they were interchangeable parts sitting on a machinery shelf. He'll stress the importance of resource planning to manage the budget and schedule. He'll plead with his bosses for more resources to enlarge the capacity of his department. The leader is the machinist, and his resources are his machine parts.

How You Treat People Determines the Results You Get

A single-minded focus on results often leads directly to treating people poorly. The drive to achieve results becomes the leader's excuse for toughness. She'll say things like, "Sure, I'm tough. We're under relentless pressure from our competitors, and margins are tight. Being tough creates urgency and motivates people to work hard. My boss is tough on me, so why shouldn't I be tough on the people who work for me?"

To be sure, results matter. But people achieve those results, and when you treat people poorly you'll get poor results. This brings us back to the central question: Do you care about me? The answer shows up in your treatment of people. You may say that you care about people, but if you never smile, constantly move up deadlines, rarely ask for their opinions or use their input, take credit for their good work, set unrealistic goals, and never say "thank you" for hard work, then you don't really care about them. And they know it.

So what does caring look like? When you care about people, you take an interest in their career aspirations. You seek, and value, their opinions. You appreciate that each person has a life outside the office that impacts how they perform inside the office. You know that people aren't just "resources"; they are the coach of a local soccer team, a lay minister at the church, an active alumna at the state college, or a husband whose wife just died after a long battle with breast cancer, and father to three heartbroken kids.

Answering "yes" to the core do-you-care-about-me question means taking a deep and genuine interest in those you are leading. Caring, in this sense, is obliging. When you care about people, you give them more of your time, attention, and active support. A wise leader treats people as more important than results, because strong people produce those results. Period.

Caring Begets Caring

As a practical matter, it's a good idea to care about your people. When they know you care about them, they will care about you—and your success. In fact, you'll know that you're truly a leader who cares when the people you lead start seeking and valuing *your* input, when they take an interest in *your* career aspirations, and when they are actively supportive of *you*. And when your people care about you, they'll help you get better results.

Much of this book is about the metaphorical doors that open-door leaders create for the people they lead. But there's one more door that you have to open before you can fully call yourself an open-door leader: the door to your heart. The people you lead need to see that behind whatever shell you portray lives an imperfect being just like them. They need to know that, despite whatever successes you've achieved, whatever power you've amassed, and whatever perks you get, you're still "real." They want to know that however big your britches are, you still have a sympathetic heart that they will always be able to reach. As long as people know that you have a good and open heart, they will let you push them, give them tough feedback, and ask them to do more. Power works best when it's anchored in humility.

Head Smooshing to Show You Care

Some people just aren't the feeling type. That doesn't mean they don't care. They just don't show their caring through their emotions. My son, Ian, for example, is not a touchy-feely little tyke. On the contrary, he's a rough-'n'-tumble boy, often with mud on his face and dirt on his feet, who tends to shy away from sentimental stuff. For example, one day when Ian was jumping on our backyard trampoline with his brother and sister, Alex and Bina, I called down from our deck to let them know I was going away on a business trip. I said, "I love you, kids!" Bina responded, "I love you too, Daddy!" Then Alex chimed in, "I love you too, Daddy!" Then Ian said, "I love your shirt, Dad!"

Like many people, Ian is uncomfortable showing his emotions, and that's perfectly fine. Unlike his brother and sister, Ian has never been one to come up and spontaneously kiss me on the cheek. However, sometimes he does slap both of my cheeks, pull my face toward his, grit his teeth, and smoosh his forehead into mine as hard as he can. I consider this his way of showing me that he cares.

The important thing is to show your caring heart in whatever way you can. Just make sure you check with HR before smooshing somebody's head.

Showing That You Care

Showing how much you care doesn't come easy for some leaders, especially the more introverted or analytical types. Keep it simple, and let your actions speak louder than your words. Don't just tell people you care about them, show them! Here are some real-life examples.

The owner of a Chicago-based highway construction business makes it a point to visit his night crews during the largest and worst snowstorms. Having come up through the ranks, he knows that crews respect you more when you show that you care about them, especially when it would be more convenient not to.

A partner at a law firm regularly takes starting lawyers out to lunch, but instead of taking them to a fancy restaurant downtown, he takes them to the downhome barbeque place by the railroad tracks next to a prison. Why? It loosens them up—you literally have to drape your necktie over your shoulder so it doesn't fall into the sloppy food! The lunches help the partner get to know his people in an informal way.

The CIO of a large office management company catches people off guard by beginning the annual strategic planning meeting in an unexpected way. He stands in front of the 12 executives and looks each one in the eye while telling them why he is grateful they are a member of his team. The CIO happens to be a painfully introverted technologist, so being this socially vulnerable is extremely uncomfortable. But he does it anyway. As he goes on, both he and his team well up with emotion. It's clear that he deeply cares about them.

The owner of a successful event management company takes her staff on a yearly "sanity" outing. Each outing is held at a different resort, which is chosen based on the quality of its spa. She makes sure her team is thoroughly and luxuriously pampered. Managing large-scale events is insanely demanding, and by taking care of her staff, she ensures that they will take care of her business (and customers).

Tough Like an M&M

One of my former bosses, Dick, wasn't some touchy-feely, bleeding heart organization-development wimp and he wasn't the type to wear his emotions on his sleeve. So it was hard to know whether he cared about me, or whether I should care about him.

After hanging up my Speedo and retiring from the U.S. High Diving Team, I got my first "real" job working for High Performing Systems, a leadership-development consulting firm based in Athens, Georgia. My boss, Dick Thompson, was a no-nonsense ex-military officer who had done two tours in Vietnam and had been decorated for heroism multiple times as a member of the elite Green Berets. While I greatly admired Dick, I was very intimidated by him. He was tough, quiet, and intense. He walked with an iron-rod posture, talked in a concise and clipped manner, and could stare right through you when he was upset. Dick was a Southern Baptist who held a black belt in karate—which meant that I worked for someone who could literally kill me with his bare hands if he wanted to and believed that God would be on his side if he did.

One day Dick and I set out on a two-hour drive up to the mountains of north Georgia. We were going to lead a three-day adventure-based leadership-development program with an international forest resource company. Dick and I would be co-facilitating, and much of the training event would be spent wearing army fatigues. I was thrilled at the prospect of working side by side with someone who knew so much about leadership—not just from textbooks (Dick had a PhD in psychology), but from years spent in the trenches leading teams in do-or-die situations. It still bugged me, however, that I didn't have any sense of who he was behind his rigid exterior.

Then Dick did something that helped me see him in a totally different light. As he turned the ignition key, he turned to me and said, "Would you mind if I put on a little music for the drive?" Thinking that I was about to get a two-hour dose of old-timey gospel music, I answered unenthusiastically, "Fine with me." Then to my pleasant surprise, the screeching guitar notes of Creedence Clear-water Revival's famous Vietnam War song, "Run Through the Jungle," came pelting through the car speakers. With that, Dick hit the gas pedal, leaving a small patch of rubber on the pavement.

For the next two hours, with John Fogerty singing in the background, Dick and I talked about his days in the battlefield fighting the Viet Cong. He opened up to me, sharing stories about what it was like to be a member of the Special Forces. I learned that he had spent much of his time in covert operations behind enemy lines. He talked about what leadership meant to him and how his Vietnam experience had influenced and shaped those ideas. He told me what it felt like to be responsible for people's lives, not in some abstract way, but literally. Dick talked about the strong bonds that formed when he and his teammates faced firefights together, and how the pain would linger for weeks after a teammate was killed. The more we talked, the more open Dick got; and the more he revealed to me, the more I appreciated him as a human being and not just as my boss.

Dick Thompson was like many proud leaders. Like an M&M candy, they're hard and crusty on the outside but sweet and soft on the inside. Sure, he was intense and a little hard to get to know, but once he opened up, you learned that he was honest, decent, and good to the core. Most people are, it just takes getting to know them to see their inherent goodness. Dick wasn't just my boss; he was a human being who had had some hard and amazing life experiences. He was someone I could admire, learn from, and listen to rock 'n' roll with.

Opening Yourself

When relationships become more personal, people usually care more. For a leader, that caring comes with a risk. When you care about people, you become more sensitive to their needs and their interests and opinions become harder to dismiss or ignore. Real relationships are obliging. Some leaders fear that by caring for others, they'll lose objectivity or independence and be taken advantage of in the process. These risks do exist, but the danger is greater if a leader is remote, aloof, and rigid. When you're as accessible as a stone obelisk, your people will secretly wish for your failure. Conversely, when people care about you as a leader, they'll strive harder to help you succeed. Regardless of the reservations you may have, you can't be an open-door leader without opening up to your people. I've listed a few simple starting points below and you can find more in the Actions and Reflections section at the end of the chapter.

- Get out of your office. Don't cloister, walk the halls, and dedicate a few hours each day to not looking at a screen of any sort.

- Smile more. People won't approach you if you're a perpetual grump.

- Set up and post a LinkedIn profile so people can view your educational background and career history if they want to.

- Display a few pictures from your life outside work and/or your family.

- If your company sponsors a softball league or folks get together for trivia night, join in the fun. Participating in casual activities should help defrost you.

- Use these words liberally and sincerely: "thank you."

Do these things even if you're uncomfortable. Strike that. Do them especially if you're uncomfortable. Remember that doing uncomfortable things is how you grow.

Open-Door Actions and Reflections

1. Reflect on the core question, "Do you care about me?"

    - Do you think your boss does or doesn't care about you? Why?

2. Now think about the people working for you.

   - Do you honestly care about them?

   - How do you think they would answer that question?

   - What evidence would they provide?

3. Are there some employees that you care about more than others?

   - Why?

   - What would have to happen for you to take a greater interest in the people you care about the least?

4. Think of a leader you've worked for who was hard to get to know at first.

   - What happened that eventually helped you see the leader differently?

   - Before getting to know him or her, did you think the leader cared about you?

   - How about after getting to know him or her?

5. How much of your non-work identity do you reveal to the people you lead?

   - What are the benefits of being more open with them?

   - What would it take for you to let them see the "real" you?

6. Put yourself, and later your team, through a personality survey like the MBTI or DiSC profile. Understand what makes you tick . . . and what ticks you off.

7. Have a "Bring an Object to Work Day."

    • Get each team member, including yourself, to bring an object from home that best reflects "what you're all about."

8. Start checking in with people, not on them.

    • Ask, "How are you doing?" not "How is the project coming along?"

    • Show them that you care about them beyond what they're getting done for you.

Conclusion

Leading Door to Door

The circle of open-door leadership is extended when the people you've opened doors for start opening doors for others. The sweetest reward is having a door opened for you by someone who's become a leader with your help.

One of my favorite career moments happened 20 years after I worked with Dick Thompson, the Vietnam vet I mentioned in the last chapter. Through the encouragement and support of open-door leaders like Dick, I started my own leadership-development company—Giant Leap Consulting. A few years ago, one of my clients wanted to conduct a workshop on how to lead during stressful times. Guess who I called? Yep, Dick Thompson.

Two decades after learning about leadership from Dick, I hired him to conduct a stress-management workshop for a group of leaders I was leading. I opened a door for a guy who had opened so many doors for me. And why not? I knew him well and had confidence in the job he'd do. He was suited for the opportunity (he had done two stressful tours in Vietnam and written a book, *The Stress Effect*). It was easy to envision how thrilled the participants would be to hear from a true hero, and I looked forward to giving him all the support he needed to be successful.

My favorite part of this moment was being able to honor Dick by introducing him to the group, and telling everyone, including Dick, how much I cared about him and how grateful I was to have learned from someone who genuinely cared about me. I was a better professional and a better human being for having worked with him.

The legacy of open-door leadership is more open-door leadership. When leaders open doors of opportunity for others, they make lasting impacts on people who can then open doors of opportunity for others. Leadership isn't some complex and abstract concept. It's a simple tradition. Leadership is a set of practices and ideals that we pass from one person to another, across organizations and generations. It's a tradition that makes people's lives better by creating opportunities for them to thrive, achieve, and lead. We all share in the rich tradition of leadership when our efforts stay directed on one thing: continually opening doors for each other.

A Final Action

Taking into account all you've read about open-door leadership, what specific actions will you take to be an open-door leader? Write your answer on a piece of paper and make sure to include a timeline to hold your feet to the fire.

Epilogue

I recently heard a story that wonderfully expresses what has come into sharp focus for me since I first wrote *Leaders Open Doors*. I heard the story along with 300 other captivated employees at the University of Michigan. I was giving a keynote talk on open-door leadership, when I asked for a volunteer to share a story about a leader who had opened a door of opportunity for him. Clarence, a burly linebacker of a man, offered to tell his story.

Ten years earlier Clarence had been the manager of a 200-room hotel. He and his wife were invited to an association meeting where, by chance, he was seated next to the general manager of a large convention hotel. The two hit it off, bonding over stories and frustrations. At the end of the evening, Clarence decided to give the GM his business card, hoping that something might come of it.

The GM, apparently, saw potential in him—the chance dinner encounter led to the GM giving Clarence the opportunity to manage a 1,000-room hotel.

The fact that a leader would take such a big risk on someone he had just met is only half of the story. The most powerful part came when I asked Clarence what that leader meant to him. Clarence, who until this point had been quite expressive, couldn't say a thing. As the seconds passed, the audience was transfixed in silence, sensing that something emotional was surfacing for Clarence. Finally, with his voice cracking and his eyes welling up, a barely audible Clarence said, "Pancreatic cancer . . . a few years later." He had to stop to wipe his eyes.

After regaining his composure, he said, "That was over 10 years ago. I swear to you, I think of him every day. I am just grateful I got to work for someone like that."

Since this book was first released, I have been honored to hear similar stories over and over again. The universal sentiment that people have when recalling a leader who opened doors for them is *gratitude*. Leaders who take an interest in our potential, help us believe in ourselves, and who take a chance on us, leave us better off then they found us. They raise our confidence, performance, and standards. Good leaders help us become better people and for that, we are profoundly grateful.

Gratitude Inspires Attitude

What has been most gratifying and unexpected about *Leaders Open Doors* is the positive twofold impact it often has on people. First, it gets people thinking about the leaders who have made a difference in their lives. A number of people have told me that the book inspired them to seek out their open-door leaders just to say "thank you."

The second impact is equally, and perhaps even more, important. After reflecting on the open-door leaders in their lives, readers then start to consider what kind of leader they are being. Many resolve to take a more active interest in supporting and advancing the careers of those they lead, and end up becoming better leaders in the process. One's leadership legacy isn't forged by having sharp elbows of ambition, but by offering caring hands to help lighten the load of others. When you do right by others, they'll do right by you.

Leaders Open Doors, Opens Doors

When I completed the first manuscript for this book, something seemed to be missing. I had said everything I wanted to say, but somehow the book felt incomplete. In the same way that it now causes people to reflect on the kind of leader they are being, the book had made me realize that for too much of my life I had been focused on me. So, I decided that writing a book about serving and empowering others without personally doing the same would be incongruent.

I realized that the best way for *Leaders Open Doors* to embody its own message would be to use it to open doors for others in a tangible and literal sense. So, I decided to donate 100 percent of the royalties that I received to charities that support children with special needs. It is a cause that is very personal for me. I have a daughter who has cerebral palsy and is deaf. She has taught me more about patience, courage, gratitude, and just plain goodness than anyone I have ever known.

Within six months of the book's initial release, I was able to make a sizable donation to the Irene Wortham Center, a charity serving severely disabled Americans in Asheville, North Carolina, as well as smaller donations to Camp Courage, which provides recreational opportunities for people with disabilities, and the March of Dimes, which is dedicated to preventing premature births—a major cause of disabilities. For the first time since its founding over a decade ago, Giant Leap Consulting donated more to charity than it made in profits. I am grateful that *Leaders Open Doors* is doing what it set out to do: open doors of opportunity for others.

The book has taught me that good things come back to you when you stop focusing on yourself and start focusing on empowering others. In the short time since the book was released I have been invited to speak at high profile conferences and events, I have been befriended by numerous renowned leadership thinkers, and I have met three astronauts. Just this past week I got invited to attend spring training for a Major League Baseball team—the general manager is kicking off the season by giving the team and staff a copy of the book. More importantly, I have had the privilege to hear countless stories about extraordinary leaders by everyday people like Clarence. Donating my royalties to charity has proven to be very enriching!

Something else has happened since *Leaders Open Doors* was originally released, too. This edition has a new publisher, ASTD Press, which is the publishing arm of The American Society for Training & Development. They view the book as a terrific leadership training vehicle, and are fully committed to giving it a bigger platform. As one of the top leadership training organizations in the world, ASTD will be able to introduce *Leaders Open Doors* to more aspiring leaders. How cool is that?

Leaders Who've Opened Doors for Leaders

I'd like to end this epilogue with some stories about open-door leadership from people who I look up to and admire. Many are well-known leadership writers. But, like Clarence, they have all been blessed by someone who left them better off than they were found. As you'll see, they're full of gratitude for the leaders who opened doors for them. As you read their stories, I'd like you to hold in your mind and heart the leaders who've opened doors for you along the way. Please send your stories to me (btreasurer@giantleap consulting.com). I'd love to hear them! Then get set on opening doors for others!

Jim Kouzes's Open-Door Leader

"You can't do it alone." That's what Don Bennett, the first amputee to climb Mt. Rainier, told me nearly 30 years ago when I asked him to share the most important lesson he learned from his ascent to the top of that mountain. It's the most important lesson I've learned from three decades of researching leadership, and it's one I keep relearning every day. I know that I could not have done what I've done without the mentoring, teaching, and counseling of so many others in my career and life.

I learned this lesson most personally from my good friend, colleague, and co-author, Barry Posner, with whom I've been researching and writing since 1982. When I first arrived on the campus of Santa Clara University as the new director of the Executive Development Center in the fall of 1981, I knew only the dean who had hired me. I was a stranger to the campus even though I'd lived and worked not far away for 10 years. On my first day, I was unpacking boxes and setting up my office when I heard a knock on my door.

I turned and saw this tall guy standing there, and he said, "Welcome to Santa Clara. My name is Barry Posner, and if you need anyone to show you around and introduce you to some of the faculty and staff just let me know." I took Barry up on his offer. Not too long after that, we found out that we had some common academic interests and Barry invited me to co-author a paper with him and Warren Schmidt on how shared values make a difference. Again, I took him up on the offer.

To make a very long story very short, 30-plus years of collaboration began because someone with a welcoming heart knocked on my door and asked if I needed help. All these years later that experience continues to teach me important lessons. Two in particular stand out. First, relationships begin when you take the initiative to make them happen. You have to knock on some doors if you want to engage with others. Second, when someone knocks on your door and offers help, say, "Yes." Yes starts things. Yes gets things moving. Yes engages.

You'll have to excuse me now. I think I hear a knock on my door.

Jim Kouzes is the co-author with Barry Posner of the best-selling book, The Leadership Challenge, *and is the Dean's Executive Fellow of Leadership at Leavey School of Business, Santa Clara University.*

Ken Blanchard's Open-Door Leader

When I was studying for my PhD, all my professors told me that if I wanted to work at a university I should be an administrator, not faculty, because I couldn't write—and I believed them. My first university job was as an administrative assistant to Dean Harry Evarts at the college of business at Ohio University. When I joined his staff, Dean Evarts asked me to teach a course in the management department, which was headed up by a man named Paul Hersey, who had also just arrived on campus.

After teaching for a few weeks, I came home and told my wife Margie, "This is what I ought to be doing. Teaching is fun."

She said, "But what about the writing?"

"I don't know, but we'll figure something out," I replied.

That fall I heard about a great leadership course Hersey was teaching, so I asked him if I could sit in on it the following semester.

"Nobody audits my course," was Hersey's response. "If you want to take it for credit, you're welcome." And he walked away. I thought that was interesting, because I had my doctorate degree and he didn't! I went home and told Margie about the conversation.

"Is he any good?" she asked.

"He's supposed to be fabulous."

"Then why don't you get your ego out of the way and take his course?"

So I did and it was a great experience.

In June 1967, after the course had ended, Hersey came to my office and said, "Ken, I've been teaching leadership for 10 years now and I think I'm better than anybody—but they want me to write a management textbook and I can't write. I've been looking for a good writer like you. Would you write it with me?"

I laughed and said, "Why not? We ought to make quite a team. You can't write and I'm not supposed to."

That's exactly what we did. Our textbook, *Management of Organizational Behavior: Utilizing Human Resources*, recently came out in its 10th edition. It sells more today than it did in the 1960s.

So it was Harry Evarts who launched my teaching career and Paul Hersey who launched my writing career. I'll be indebted to them both forever.

Ken is the chief spiritual officer of The Ken Blanchard Companies and author of more than 50 books, including The One Minute Manager.

John H. "Jack" Zenger's Open-Door Leader

I had just finished an MBA degree at UCLA and was working in my first job. After a year and a few months, I was contacted by Mike Blansfield to come to work with him in the management development department of the Pacific Finance Corporation, a Transamerica company. Mike was an early pioneer in organization development and he gave me the opportunity to work closely with Dick Beckhard, Herb Shepherd, Robert Blake, and other early pioneers in this new discipline. This opened my eyes to the world of consulting and I was inspired by what these people did for organizations. I wanted to make that impact on organizations and most of these consultants had been academics, so I was motivated to go back to school to get a doctoral degree.

Mike's willingness to take a chance with a totally inexperienced young guy with an MBA led me down a path that totally transformed my life in a permanent way.

Jack is the co-founder and CEO of Zenger Folkman and co-author of five leadership books, including The Extraordinary Leader.

Beverly Kaye's Open-Door Leader

Many years ago, before I entered this field, I had a wonderful opportunity to study at the Sloan School of Management at MIT, as a special student in their organization development track. At that time I was an assistant dean of students at Brandeis University and I had been attending classes at Sloan on a unique exchange program.

One of my professors was Dick Beckhard, who was considered "the father of OD." I had read his writings and was in awe of his work, as well as his role and impact on a field that fascinated me and that I wanted to follow. During this class, we all had to write a paper, and we had to make a 15-minute appointment with Dick to review the direction of our paper.

When my turn came to schedule my slot, I was unable to fit into the schedule because of my work at Brandeis. So, Dick offered to meet with me over dinner, and when I said that wouldn't work, he looked me in the eye and insisted on the truth. I explained that in 15 minutes I thought I could look smart enough, but over an entire dinner I would never be able to hold up my end of the conversation.

Of course we ended up going to dinner, and it turned into a wonderful mentoring relationship that lasted for many years. I think it was his influence that led me to pursue my doctorate and to believe that I had something to offer this field.

Beverly Kaye is founder and chairwoman of Career Systems International and the author of four books, including Love 'Em or Lose 'Em.

Kevin Eikenberry's Open-Door Leader

I've been blessed to have many leaders who have made a difference and opened doors for me and my future. But none more than my father, Phil Eikenberry.

Dad, was of course my father, but he was also my first boss. We farmed and had an agricultural-related business and I was given responsibility for leadership, customer service, and more from a very early age. This too, might not be completely unusual in this context, except for the degree of my responsibilities. Here's just one example: Customers were informed that if they got answers from me, they were final. People couldn't "go around" me to Dad and get a different answer. If they did, the first question he asked was, "What did Kevin say?"

This level of responsibility and trust not only built confidence and skills, but set an example that I hope I follow and teach every day. When we believe in those we lead, and show them through our actions, it makes a lasting difference.

Do you believe in those you lead and if so, are you showing them?

Kevin Eikenberry is chief potential officer of The Kevin Eikenberry Group, and author of two bestselling books, including Remarkable Leadership.

Elaine Biech's Open-Door Leader

Too often we underestimate the power of believing in someone. Another's confidence in you has the potential to ignite an exciting future. Many people believed in me throughout my career, but two of the earliest made the greatest difference in my life: Bill Williams and Matt Holt.

Bill Williams, personnel director for NASA Langley Research Center, hired me to design a meeting management training program. But it wasn't just any run-of-the-mill, stand-up training session. It was going to be used as the basis for the first video teleconference prototype beamed (as Bill would say) to all the NASA sites around the country. His trust in me to design and deliver a typical learning session for an atypical and untested medium was exhilarating. It was my personal "5, 4, 3, 2, 1, Liftoff!" It still seems inconceivable to me that NASA trusted an unknown trainer from a farm in Wisconsin with this significant task.

Matt Holt, currently an executive editor for John Wiley & Sons, encouraged me to write *The Business of Consulting*. At the time, all I had was a stack of scribbled ideas written on notecards, scraps of paper, and napkins. Matt seemed as excited about the book as I was, giving me a double dose of self-confidence and a desire to succeed. This has now become my model for starting every book I've published since.

Both of these gentlemen believed in me, and those two projects led me to do the kind of incredibly exciting work that continues to fuel my passion: writing, creating, and developing others. Believing in someone is the most valuable gift you can give another.

Elaine Biech is the president and managing principle of ebb associates and author or editor of more than 50 books, including The ASTD Leadership Handbook.

Mark Sanborn's Open-Door Leader

I've never liked conflict—who does? But long before I served on the board of directors for the National Speakers Association, then president, Naomi Rhode, asked me to deal with a conflict situation.

"You have just the right temperament to do this," she said.

While I wasn't keen on dealing with conflict between myself and another person, I found that I was a pretty good mediator for others, and a stabilizing influence in the type of situation Naomi had asked me to handle. The problem was resolved successfully.

Naomi saw something in me I didn't see in myself. And that is a sign of great leadership.

Mark Sanborn is the president of Sanborn and Associates and author of eight books, including You Don't Need a Title to Be a Leader.

Chip Bell's Open-Door Leader

I was a new training director for a large bank and fresh out of grad school. After settling into my new role, I started a search for an assistant training director. The candidate that caught my attention had been a supervisory trainer in the Coast Guard and—this is the part that really impressed me—had gotten his master's degree at a prestigious Ivy League college after the military.

I was eager to make him an offer almost as soon as he arrived for a day of interviews. But my boss, Chuck, who had been a recruiter for a large manufacturing company before joining the bank, had big reservations.

"I think he's all hat and no cows!" Chuck said. But I had Ivy League stars in my eyes.

"What do you recommend I do?" I asked him when it came time to make the offer (or not).

"I wouldn't hire him," was Chuck's direct answer. "But, it's your decision and I will support whatever you decide."

I hired the guy. And, six months later, I fired him. He was all about form and not results. My boss never said a word about my bad decision. It was a powerful lesson I have never forgotten. Chuck practiced the belief that the worth of profound learning more than outweighed the price of an occasional error.

Chip Bell is founder and senior partner with the Chip Bell Group and author of more than 20 books, including Managers as Mentors *(co-authored with Marshall Goldsmith).*

Verne Harnish's Open-Door Leader

An open-door leader who comes to my mind is Arthur Lipper, former owner of *Venture Magazine.* I had recently co-founded the Association of Collegiate Entrepreneurs (ACE), but we needed some national traction. So I drove down from Wichita to Dallas, where I had read that Arthur was giving a speech.

Afterward, I cornered him, shared what I was trying to accomplish, and asked him for his advice. Long story short, Arthur became a key mentor. Each year he donated a page in his magazine to our organization, which provided the air cover we needed; he opened his rolodex to speakers for our events; he trusted me with his two teenagers when I led a delegation of young entrepreneurs to China in 1986; and he came to my defense in a serious situation that could have derailed the organization and my reputation.

Thirty years later, Arthur remains a friend and mentor (he and his wife just visited us in Barcelona a few months ago) and I can say without a doubt that I wouldn't be doing what I am today without his early and ongoing support.

Verne Harnish is the founder of Entrepreneur's Organiza-tion (EO), founder and CEO of Gazelles, and author of two books, including Mastering the Rockefeller Habits.

BJ Gallagher's Open-Door Leader

Years ago when I was working at the University of Southern California College of Continuing Education, academic prior-ities were changing and continuing education was being decentralized to the individual schools and colleges. This all meant that my job was going to be phased out. Around the same time, I saw a director of training and organization development job advertised in the campus newspaper, and thought, "*That's for me!*"

I applied and was given an opportunity to interview—more as a courtesy than anything, since Gary Gould, the faculty member doing the hiring, already had a favored candidate. But during that courtesy interview, I must have said the right things, because I could see that Gould was becoming more interested in me as a serious candidate. Bottom line: He hired me for the job.

What I didn't know until months later was that he didn't hire me for my experience—he hired me for my *potential*. When he hired me, he told his boss, the VP of administration, "She doesn't know shit about training, but she sure can light up a room!"

What I brought to the job was charisma, outstanding interpersonal skills, creativity, and initiative, as well as the willingness to embark on a steep learning curve. By this point I had been at USC for almost 10 years and had built up a robust network of professional relationships with faculty and staff, whereas Gould was new to campus. I had strong financial skills, good organizational abilities, and was superb at marketing classes and workshops. In other words, I had valuable generic talents, skills, and experience to offer—and my new boss was willing teach me what I didn't know about training and development.

I'll always be grateful to him for giving me a chance, even when he'd already made up his mind to hire someone else. His open-mindedness changed the course of my career, and I've been in the training and development business ever since. And 30 years later, some say I can still light up a room.

BJ Gallagher is the president of Peacock Productions and co-author of A Peacock in the Land of Penguins *and* Being Buddha At Work.

Acknowledgments

Countless doors were opened for me while I was writing this book. I am especially grateful to the many author and client friends who took the time to review early drafts of the manuscript and gave me invaluable improvement suggestions. Especially useful feedback came from Chip Bell, BJ Gallagher, Sharon Jordan-Evans, Mark Levy, Maren Showkeir, Charles Lang, and Naomi George.

Nancy Breuer served as my Virgil as I navigated through writing this book. She mentored, educated, and cajoled me into writing a better book than the one I first shared with her. She's a wonderful editor with whom to share a book journey.

I am especially grateful to Glenn Saltzman, Ann Parker, Melissa Jones, and many other wonderful people at ASTD Press for believing in the book and its potential. Dawn Baron of Passion Profits Consulting, deserves a special thanks for all the ways she supports me and my work. Thank you Dawn!

Becky Robinson and the publicity virtuosos at Weaving Influence helped trumpet this book far and wide. Bravo! Encore!

I continue to be indebted to my wonderful clients. They've provided me with a meaningful and fulfilling career. I am always grateful when clients become true friends and I hesitate to name specific people for fear of excluding or forgetting anyone. Some do, however, deserve special recognition, namely, Mike Calihan, Craig Atkinson, the Aldridge family, Steve Rivi, Sandra Alexander, Gail Tolbert, Naomi George, Thomas Schwerzmann, Marie Guevara, Tina Meyer, and Lynn Morgan.

Giant Leap Consulting has now been around for more than a decade and it would have gone off the rails years ago were it not for the wonderful courage, commitment, and ownership of current and former Giant Leapers, including Laura Cohn, Becky Jarrell, Ahli Moore, Michelle Sissine, Justine Foo, and Charles Lang.

I love my children and they love me. What more can a parent ask for? Being a father to Alex, Bina, and Ian has made me a richer and better person. Much of what I do, I do because of my love for them. I love you, kids! I am proud of you!

Having written is easier than writing. Writers, including me, can be a little moody during the writing process. I think my wife would agree, though, that this book put me in a better and lighter mood than my previous books did. Thankfully my wife has become quite experienced at living with me when I'm in "writer mode." I love you, Shannon!

Finally, I would like to thank all the dead people! I am a spiritual guy, and I am grateful to those friends and loved ones who have traveled beyond life's veil. I am especially grateful to my grandmother, GooGoo. I grew up a lower-middle-class kid in an upper-class town. GooGoo always taught me to hold my chin up high. Thank you for blessing me with your Irish, Nordic, Celtic spirit!

About the Author

Bill Treasurer is the founder and chief encouragement officer at Giant Leap Consulting, a company that exists to help people and organizations live more courageously. He is widely regarded as the originator of the new organizational-development practice of courage building.

Bill is the author of the internationally bestselling book *Courage Goes to Work*, which provides practical strategies for inspiring more courageous behavior in workplace settings. He is also the creator of a do-it-yourself leadership-training program, *Courageous Leadership: Using Courage to Transform the Workplace*. The program promotes managerial courage and has been taught to thousands of executives throughout the world. Learn more at www.pfeiffer.com/go/courage.

Since 1991 Bill has led more than 500 corporate workshops and webinars for notable clients including NASA, Saks Fifth Avenue, Accenture, Monster.com, Bank of America, CNN, SPANX, the Center for Creative Leadership, Hugo Boss, UBS Bank, PNC Bank, the U.S. Forest Service, the National Science Foundation, and the U.S. Department of Veterans Affairs. Learn more at www.couragebuilding.com.

Bill's insights have been featured in more than 100 newspapers—including *Washington Post, New York Daily News, Chicago Tribune, Atlanta Journal Constitution, Boston Herald,* and *Investor's Business Daily*—as well as many magazines, including *Leader to Leader, Leadership Excellence, Business-to-Business, Parents Magazine, Redbook, Women's Day, Training Magazine,* and the *Harvard Management Update.*

Prior to founding Giant Leap Consulting, Bill was an executive in change management and human performance practice at Accenture, a $28 billion management consulting firm. He became Accenture's first fulltime internal executive coach and coached Accenture senior executives to become more courageous leaders.

Bill's first book, *Right Risk,* is about how to take smart risks. As a former captain of the U.S. High Diving Team, he traveled throughout the world for seven years with a team of high-performing athletes. During that time, he did more than 1,500 dives from heights that scaled to over 100 feet . . . sometimes on fire!

Bill received a master of science degree from the University of Wisconsin after graduating from West Virginia University on a full athletic scholarship. He serves as board chairman for Leadership Asheville, is on the board of his local YMCA, and fights for the rights of people with disabilities, including his daughter, Bina.

You can contact Bill at btreasurer@giantleapconsulting .com, follow him on Twitter (@btreasurer), connect on LinkedIn (www.linkedin.com/in/courage), or find him on Facebook (http://facebook.com/bill.treasurer). For more information about this book, visit www.leadersopendoors.com.

About Giant Leap Consulting

Giant Leap Consulting is on a mission to help people and organizations act with more courage. Since its founding in 2002, Giant Leap has conducted more than 500 separate client engagements related to elevating individual employee and organizational performance.

We believe that people work more effectively and with higher levels of passion and commitment when they are operating out of confidence and courage, rather than out of fear and anxiety. Our client engagements are built upon the foundational conviction that people achieve extraordinary results when they engage courageously with one another. In short, our aim is to create courageous organizations.

Giant Leap has four service lines:

- **Courageous future:** Strategic planning services designed to help organizations create a bold and compelling future.

- **Courageous leadership:** Leadership and succession-planning programs and curricula designed to create courageous leaders.

- **Courageous teaming:** High-impact team-building programs that promote honest, responsible, and adult-like behavior from all team members.

- **Courageous development:** Customized training programs that build individual skills and organizational capabilities.

Giant Leap works with profit and nonprofit organizations that aim for a higher standard of performance, including Accenture, PNC Bank, Walsh Construction, Saks Fifth Avenue, Hugo Boss, UBS Bank, and UNICEF.

Working extensively with the U.S. government, Giant Leap has consulted for the Centers for Disease Control and Prevention, the National Science Foundation, the U.S. Department of Veterans Affairs, the U.S. Army, the U.S. Forest Service, and NASA.

To learn more, visit our websites giantleapconsulting .com, couragebuilding.com, managerialcourage.com, and www.pfeiffer.com/go/courage. You can also follow Giant Leap Consulting on Twitter (@takegiantleaps), connect on LinkedIn (www.linkedin.com/in/courage), or "Like" us on Facebook.